RAND NATIONAL DEFENSE RESEARCH INSTITUTE

T0289377

Producing Joint Qualified Officers

FY 2008 to FY 2017 Trends

Paul W. Mayberry, William H. Waggy II, Anthony Lawrence

Prepared for the Office of the Secretary of Defense

For more information on this publication, visit www.rand.org/t/RR3105

Library of Congress Cataloging-in-Publication Data is available for this publication.
ISBN: 978-1-9774-0278-3

Published by the RAND Corporation, Santa Monica, Calif.
© Copyright 2019 RAND Corporation
RAND® is a registered trademark.

Support RAND
Make a tax-deductible charitable contribution at
www.rand.org/giving/contribute

www.rand.org

Preface

Since enactment of the Goldwater-Nichols Department of Defense Reorganization Act in 1986, the Department of Defense (DoD) has continued to reform and refine its policies regarding both joint professional military education (JPME) and joint duty assignments. Once these education and duty assignments have been completed, a service member may be designated as a joint qualified officer (JQO)—aligning with a central tenet in the original legislation to increase the quality, stability, and experience of officers assigned to joint organizations with the ultimate intent of improving joint operational outcomes.

The fundamental elements for educating and managing JQOs are codified in law and implemented via DoD policy. Over time, these policies have been modified and updated to reflect operational considerations and to provide additional enhancements and flexibilities. Such changes included expanding the institutions that were eligible to provide senior-level JPME and implementing a points-based joint qualification system that recognized career-long accumulation of joint experiences, education, and training. In this report we detail the joint qualifying parameters and characterize their evolution over time.

The overall objective of this research was to quantify and assess the production of JQOs by examining trends in achieving educational requirements and accomplishing joint assignments. Similarly, we examined the evolution of policies in these areas and their influence on such trends. In this manner, we established a baseline of outcomes which allows policymakers to evaluate the impacts of both current and future policy changes. This information does not currently exist and is not systematically reviewed for implications and practices that could have cross-service benefits. The report is focused on historical trends for field grade officers (O-4 to O-6) in the active component over a ten-year time period from FY 2008 to FY 2017.

This research was sponsored by the Deputy Assistant Secretary of Defense for Force Education and Training and conducted within the Forces and Resources Policy Center of the RAND Corporation National Defense Research Institute, a federally funded research and development center sponsored by the Office of the Secretary of Defense, the Joint Staff, the Unified Combatant Commands, the U.S. Navy, the U.S. Marine Corps, the defense agencies, and the defense Intelligence Community.

For more information on the RAND Forces and Resources Policy Center, see www.rand.org/nsrd/ndri/centers/frp or contact the director (contact information is provided on the webpage).

Contents

Figures and Tables

Tables

Summary

The passage of the Goldwater-Nichols Department of Defense Reorganization Act (GNA) of 1986 resulted in significant personnel reforms in defining and developing joint officers. The fundamental GNA elements were (1) joint professional military education (JPME) in accredited joint schools; (2) a joint duty assignment list (JDAL) that required and provided application of joint knowledge; (3) designation of joint specialty officers (later changed to joint qualified officers, JQOs) for those who successfully completed an appropriate level of joint education and duty assignment; and (4) joint criteria and benchmarks associated with officer promotions.

Appreciating that the services retained the power of controlling assignment and promotion processes, referred to as joint officer management (JOM), the GNA mandated joint qualification as a prerequisite for promotion to the general and flag officer ranks, minimum tour lengths for joint billets, and a reporting system that sought to ensure compliance and reward joint experience.

The fundamental elements for educating and managing joint officers are codified in law and implemented via Department of Defense (DoD) policy. Over time, these policies have been modified and updated to reflect operational considerations and to provide additional enhancements and flexibilities. For example, revisions have expanded the institutions eligible to provide senior-level JPME and implemented a points-based joint qualification system (JQS) that recognized career-long accumulation of joint experiences, education, and training. We detail these joint qualifying parameters further and characterize their evolution over time.

The Study Approach

The overall objective of this research was to quantify and assess the production of JQOs to establish a baseline of JOM and JPME outcomes from which to assess historical trends. Such information does not currently exist and is not systematically reviewed for implications and practices that would have cross-service benefits. This report provides such historical trends for field grade officers (O-4 to O-6) in the active component over a ten-year time period from FY 2008 to FY 2017.

More specifically, we

- analyzed JQO inventories and appointees on an annual basis, examining trends by policy-relevant categories: service, grade, and occupational specialty
- examined historical JQO trends for graduates from JPME Phase II (JPME-II) granting institutions
- considered the two primary paths to achieving joint experience—a standard joint duty assignment (S-JDA) and an experience joint duty assignment (E-JDA)
- addressed the sequencing of education and duty assignment
- examined trends of waivers usage as exceptions were made to policy
- conducted two case studies to examine experiences of JQOs.

To gain a historical context and to appreciate other factors that may have contributed to trend variances, we reviewed relevant laws, policies, and regulations and engaged in discussions with the JOM and JPME offices of the services and Joint Staff. The purpose of these interactions was to better understand their perceptions on data validity, gain their historical recollections of policy and operational events that could affect JQO findings, understand their thoughts on implications of our findings, and identify potential JOM and JPME practices that may be effective for others. As policy changes generally take considerable time for effects to be realized, the trends presented in this report serve as a baseline against which to assess change, impact, and direction of effects.

What We Learned from the Trends Data

- The **inventory** of active component field grade JQOs increased considerably over the past decade, from about 5,100 to 7,300. From FY 2014 to FY 2017, the JQO inventory for each service was stable for all services except the U.S. Marine Corps, which achieved growth in all years.
- The number of active component field grade officers who were **annually appointed** as JQOs declined considerably in 2017—by over 250 in total across all the military services. The greatest decline was experienced by the U.S. Air Force, but all services showed a noticeable drop. It is not evident if the recent decline in appointees is a trend or a reflection of considerable annual variance.
- The number and percentage of O-6 JQOs have exceeded outcomes for all other **grades** in nearly all years. Differences over time and between grades show that the services have different philosophies toward talent management of their field grade officers.
- While the services differed in relative portions of their officer corps that serve in tactical operations **occupations**, all showed higher portions of their tactical operations officers qualified as JQOs. Over the last ten years, the consistently

increasing percentage of tactical operations officers who have become JQOs was striking. However, the services differed in the magnitude of increases.

- Over the last ten years, around 1,600 **JPME-II degrees** have been conferred annually. The Joint and Combined Warfighting School (JCWS) has produced about 55 percent of all JPME-II graduates. The senior joint schools (SJSs) and senior service schools (SSSs) also produced constant percentages—about 17–20 percent and 25–29 percent, respectively. For O-4s and O-5s, the services predominantly used the JCWS. Service utilization of different institutions became even more apparent when focusing on O-6s.

- After an initial lag associated with implementing the points-based JQS in FY 2007, the percentage of individuals achieving JQO designation via the E-JDA path climbed quickly. In recent years, the numbers have stabilized at around 16 percent. Services have made differential use of the two **paths for achieving joint experience**, and such differences are only accentuated across grade.

- The services employed various approaches for **sequencing** JPME-II with an S-JDA tour. The JCWS was the only option available for officers to receive education during the course of their assignment. In the case of SJSs, approximately 60 percent of their graduates completed degrees prior to joint assignment. Conversely, 65 percent of SSS graduates who received JPME-II credit did so after they finished their joint assignment. Only the Marine Corps tended to send greater portions of its officers to JPME-II prior to assignment. Relatively few O-4s and junior O-5s attended JPME-II prior to a tour. This is an interesting finding in that such junior officers are most likely in need of preparations in joint matters given their limited career histories.

- The use of tour length curtailment **waivers** is intended to be for exceptional circumstances only. The percentage of waivers granted annually had minor variability around 10 percent. These waivers were used in greater numbers for higher-grade individuals going into command assignments. The U.S. Air Force and Army made greatest use of these waivers.

Observations and Implications

The Need for Authoritative Data and a Comparison Baseline

All service and Joint Staff stakeholders acknowledged the value but also the limitations of the data system used to manage the JQO production process and lamented the need for a more accurate and authoritative information source. We are aware that the Office of the Secretary of Defense (OSD) is in the process of procuring system enhancements. Close coordination and feedback from JOM and JPME stakeholders will be essential to ensure that their past difficulties and future information needs are sufficiently addressed.

Historically, the services, Joint Staff, OSD, and U.S. Congress have viewed annual reports that offered a limited view of the JQO process. By examining only a single year, the reports provided no basis for assessing either magnitude or consistency. During our conversations, all parties recognized the value of a multiyear perspective. The data and methods employed in this report provide a consistent analytical basis for defining variables, describing concepts, and calculating trends. This longer-term outlook allowed subject matter experts to notice effects that were not readily apparent from a single-year snapshot and to account for the natural lags in policies taking effect and their outcomes being realized. Stakeholders also valued JQO trend comparisons across services. They were interested in determining what policies or implementation approaches may have benefit for their respective services.

Finally, the services desired a common historical baseline to assist their efforts in determining and assessing the future impact of policy changes. Specifically, they understood the considerable number and magnitude of policy adjustments implemented with the revision of Department of Defense Instruction (DoDI) 1300.19 (April 3, 2018).[1] This significant policy revision highlights a number of questions for future trend analysis and research issues that necessitate a baseline for policy evaluation.

Joint Qualified Officer Production Is Stable But May Be Declining

The JQO trends over the last ten years showed that all services achieved considerable growth. However, during the FY 2015 to FY 2017 time frame, these numbers stabilized and even declined in terms of annual appointees. These declines, observed across all services except the Marine Corps, raised questions of "demand" for JQOs (an issue beyond the scope of this current study). Have the services now achieved JQO supply production totals that are sufficient to satisfy the JQO demands of joint customers? The Joint Staff conducts systematic validations of joint duty assignments that should provide insight into this critical question. Therefore, a possible decline in JQO production may not be an issue if JQO demand is being sufficiently met. Several services thought that with reductions in their respective end strengths there should be commensurate reductions in joint duty assignment requirements. Such questions are the intended focus and purpose of the Joint Staff's periodic JDAL review and validation.

JQO production has varied by service. While joint billets are distributed somewhat equally across military departments, a good number of joint positions are competitively sourced. The Army and Marine Corps increased the percentage of JQOs in their officer corps over time. However, the Air Force had the largest absolute number of JQOs. Consideration of the relative differences among the services with regard to number versus percentage of JQOs may reflect how the services manage and develop their officer corps in the intricate balance of officer quality in satisfying both service and joint assignment requirements. The net outcome of these trade-offs will be officers

---

[1]   DoDI 1300.19, *DoD Joint Officer Management (JOM) Program*, April 3, 2018.

who are able to effectively conduct and lead both service and joint operations, as well as individuals who will be competitive for selection to advantageous joint assignments and ultimately for the more coveted general and flag officer joint positions.

It is evident that the services took diverse approaches to talent management and the timing associated with gaining joint experience. For example, the Air Force developed and maintained consistently large JQO inventories composed of officers early in their careers. It may be the case that some services are attempting to delay "time away" from the service at critical junctures or career points or simply postponing joint assignments as long as possible. This approach is contrasted to an alternative approach in which the services achieve jointness later in officers' careers. This is reflected in the percentages of JQO O-6s increased considerably over time within each service. The trend was especially true for the Marine Corps: over 70 percent of its O-6s were JQOs. Another interpretation was that JQO status as an O-6 had now become an established norm in an officer's career, in much the same way that earning a master's degree has become standard. As a range of policy modifications have made additional pathways to JQO available, reasons for not being designated a JQO have become less defensible.

These observed trends could be influenced by or the result of differential service deployments over the last decade and the challenges to fully develop individuals not only as leaders but in the full scope of their warfighting requirements. Based on the limited data available, we were not able to determine if such deployments were in fact a positive influence contributing to JQO designation (through the E-JDA path) or a hindrance given the time associated with operations that were not strategically oriented toward joint matters.

Complexities in Interpreting Joint Personnel Policies Trends

Past personnel policy changes have been an attempt to better reflect the realities of joint operational demands and provide greater flexibility to accommodate service needs. At times these two objectives can be diametrically opposed or raise further questions for exploration. Some examples include:

- The joint qualification system sought credit for joint experiences by constructing equivalencies to full joint duty tours. Trends showed increased use of E-JDAs, especially for services with greater strategic joint deployment responsibilities. It is an open question as to the quality and equivalency of JQOs designated by alternative experience paths.
- Reduced tour durations from 36 to 24 months and corresponding reductions in joint qualification points were requested by the services as they argued that their command tours were typically two years. These revisions have yet to be implemented long enough to determine their impact on joint outcomes.
- JPME-II is no longer a prerequisite for a joint assignment but rather a matter of timing and availability determined by the services. It is the perspective of and

assessment by the joint community that is missing from this calculus: Are officers reporting to assignments sufficiently prepared and capable of performing their joint billet responsibilities?

- All SSSs are now accredited to provide JPME-II. An unintended outcome of this expansion is that the services are explicitly waiting until later in officers' careers to achieve simultaneously senior service and senior joint education. This results in many officers relying on JPME Phase I (JPME-I) as the only joint preparations for their joint duty assignment and the later awarding of JQO designations at higher grades.

- Based on shorter durations, more annual convenings, and greater geographical dispersion of the JCWS JPME-II program, the services made consistent and high utilization of this educational offering—to even include higher grades. The services were not able to address the question of equivalency of graduate outcomes compared with SJSs or SSSs other than the fact that all programs generated the same status as graduates.

- The trend of JQO designations at higher grades is a paradox, as the preponderance of joint duty assignments are for O-4s and junior O-5s. The policy to examine and report equity of promotion rates of joint officers versus officers assigned to service headquarters is no longer a requirement and should possibly be reconsidered given these discrepancies.

- Another interpretation of the significant and continuing increase of O-6 JQOs is that all services are strictly adhering to the legislative requirements that all officers must be so designated prior to being considered for promotion to general or flag officer. Such explicit and well-defined policy requirements appear to effectively influence service officer management behaviors.

- As the services continue to face evolving threats, the need for more advanced joint operational concepts continues to grow, and thus so does the demand for even more joint warfighters. Jointness is progressing beyond interservice capability to also include interagency, multinational, and coalition jointness for an ever expanding set of mission areas—both in space and in cyberwarfare. The existing constraints will remain, and they will play an even greater role in the development and management of joint personnel.

The fundamental question in each of these areas is the extent to which policy changes are contributing to or detracting from the ultimate objective of providing sufficient numbers and quality of joint officers. The Joint Staff and OSD—through the specification of required service metrics, annual report submissions, educational institution accreditation processes, and periodic engagements with combatant commanders—should work to assess the net outcome of policy changes on the quality of JQOs and their ability to satisfy the performance expectations of the joint community. Until such time, trend analysis can lead to a proper, albeit incomplete, discussion, vetting, and assessment of policy changes.

Joint Education Accomplished Based on Timing and Availability

With JPME policy changes that have allowed both SJSs and SSSs to confer JPME-II status, there are now a wide variety of venues to achieve the joint educational requirements—in addition to the JCSW and its recent more flexible offerings. Given differences in program duration between SJSs and SSSs (ten months) and the JCWS (ten weeks), various constituencies are beginning to question the equivalence and quality of strategic joint educational outcomes. Such questions were beyond the scope of this study, but it was evident that the JCWS (as currently defined and implemented) satisfied a considerably high portion of JPME-II educational requirements, addressed both O-4 and O-5 educational needs that cannot be satisfied by either an SJS or SSS, offered a range of flexibilities in terms of geographical satellite and hybrid offerings, and had a diversity of students and faculties that is difficult for an SSS to consistently achieve. We expect that modifications to current JCWS offerings would have greater impact on the reserve component, though this was not an explicit focus for this study.

While we did not explore the accomplishment of JPME-I, we noted that direct entry waivers were a rare exception, authorized strictly on a case-by-case basis. Therefore, in cases where officers receive JPME-II education after the completion of their S-JDA tour, they were relying completely on their JPME-I instruction as the basis for and context to performing in the joint assignment. This reliance on only intermediate JPME was the case in 65 percent, 41 percent, and 37 percent of JQOs who completed their JPME-II requirement at SSSs, SJSs, and the JCWS, respectively, after their joint duty assignment. These trends only increased over the ten-year time period that we examined and offered support for anecdotal concerns raised by joint organization leaders who have lamented the strategic ability of officers to deal with a range of joint requirements. The Chairman of the Joint Chiefs of Staff (CJCS)'s Process for Accreditation of Joint Education should examine this issue as an item of special interest.

Joint education is a lever that the services control in that the timing of education rests on service decisions and priorities. We consistently heard from the services that the sequencing of education and assignment was determined not only by the leadership intent of education preparing an officer for the rigors of a joint assignment but also by "timing and availability" for both the individual officer and the good of the service or joint organization. Because law and policy do not serve as a forcing mechanism for joint education timing, the services use pathways that support service objectives. When the service uses JQO attainment as a screening mechanism for talent management, as in the Air Force and Marine Corps, joint education often occurs near in time to a joint assignment. When SSS selection outweighs the importance of JQO attainment, joint education occurs later in an officer's career through SSSs, as in the Army. When joint education must be accomplished in as little time as possible, as in the U.S. Navy, the JCWS becomes the only viable alternative to the service.

Primary Drivers for Joint Qualified Officers Production

The joint education requirement reflects a career-long commitment to officer professional military education (PME) that spans from precommissioning to the most senior general and flag officer ranks. Such education requires the balancing of both service and joint offerings. Through Chairman of the Joint Chiefs of Staff Instruction (CJCSI) 1800.01E, the Joint Staff has detailed the standards, learning areas, and objectives that define the JPME programs for officers to be successful in joint assignments.[2] These specifications cover all ranks of field grade officers. Through the completion of successive levels of PME and JPME, field grade officers are intended to be prepared for the rigors of their joint assignments. Additionally, joint duty assignments reflect the demands of all joint commands and organizations. The demands are expressed in the JDAL, which is validated to not only reflect joint billet requirements but also the grades necessary to perform these duties. The JDAL is heavily weighted toward requirements for the more junior ranks of field grade officers. Across all services, the distribution of grades are approximately 45 percent O-4s, 35 percent O-5s, and 20 percent O-6s.

Developing both service and joint expertise within the constraint of a fixed career length has its challenges. As a result, the preferred order of education first, and then an assignment, is not always possible. As services seek to accomplish JPME increasingly through senior institutions, post assignment education will progressively become the de facto standard (as opposed to the exception), and thereby JPME-I and intermediate service PME will be the only instructional preparations for the preponderance of O-5 assignments and all O-4 billets. This raises a fundamental question regarding the educational prerequisites (if any) and preparations needed to successfully perform the duties of joint assignments, especially for junior personnel. Feedback from senior joint leadership over time will be essential to assess the impact of this transition to greater use of senior institutions. Again, this topic should be a focus item for the Process for Accreditation of Joint Education, with explicit attention on the performance outcomes of the more junior field grade officers.

Continuing to acknowledge that joint duty assignments remain an important component of an officer's development, the services stated that joint manpower demands have outpaced available officer inventories. To sustain readiness levels and to balance service manpower inventories with the need for joint requirements and officer development, the services have developed guidance that prioritizes personnel fill rates. Relative to past years, this guidance typically has adjusted joint manning levels down slightly but still maintained relatively high levels. Some services have also made differentiations between priorities for various categories of joint requirements (e.g., manning at combatant commands versus the Joint Staff).

---

[2]   CJCSI 1800.01E, *Officer Professional Military Education Policy (OPMEP)*, May 29, 2015a.

The original GNA legislation had two binding constraints that sought to define measures of congressional intent and to ensure that the services sufficiently complied: (1) comparable promotion rates for officers in joint assignments with officers in service headquarters, and (2) JQO designation prior to consideration for promotion to general and flag officer positions. The comparable promotion rate constraint was modified with the April 2018 JOM policy update and is now only reported to OSD. Conversely, general and flag officer promotion consideration has only been reinforced in the sense that waivers associated with prior education or experiential requirements are rarely granted. In fact, for two consecutive years the Marine Corps had O-6s removed from the general officer consideration who had not fully completed the JQO designation process, and waivers were denied. It was evident from the JQO trend results that reported metrics provided a strong forcing function to drive service behaviors and policies.

There is no longer a question about the criticality of jointness being central to the success of any mission conducted by DoD. The department has made tremendous advances in this regard since the initial passage of the GNA. Advancements have resulted from investments in the career-long development of officers to be proficient in joint matters and from the revision of associated policies. This research has contributed to understanding the past and current state of joint qualifications for active component field grade officers and serves as a foundation and baseline for understanding, designing, and assessing future personnel policy changes that benefit the joint force, military services, and individual officers.

Acknowledgments

We are grateful to the many people who were involved in this research. In particular, we thank our OSD sponsor, Deputy Assistant Secretary of Defense for Force Education and Training Fred Drummond, for his help and guidance throughout this study. Eric Russi, who serves as the professional military education senior adviser within the Office of the Deputy Assistant Secretary of Defense for Force Education and Training, and Lt Col Todd "Randy" Randolph, assistant director of joint officer management within the Office and Enlisted Personnel Management directorate of the Office of the Deputy Assistant Secretary of Defense for Military Personnel Policy, were very gracious with their time, expertise, and professional advice.

We are indebted to Jerry Lynes, Deputy Director of Joint Education and Doctrine of the Joint Staff J7, and Debbie Potratz of the Joint Staff J1 Human Capital Division for their extraordinary knowledge and expertise in producing joint qualified officers, as well as their openness and willingness to share that information with others. Maureen Ross of the Defense Manpower Data Center was instrumental in assisting with access to and understanding of data from the Joint Duty Assignment Management Information System.

We also acknowledge the pivotal roles played by service and Joint Staff representatives from offices associated with joint education and joint officer management: for the Air Force, Col Keithen Washington and Jacqueline Ledoux; for the Army, LTC Bryan Donohue; for the Marine Corps, Col. Leland Suttee, LtCol. Mark Nicholson, and Maj. Brian Everett; for the Navy, CDR Steven Moss, Steven Cullen, and Melerie Thompson; for Joint Staff J7, COL Tim Teague, Jerry Lynes, Jack Roesner, and Patrick Shaw; and for Joint Staff J1, CDR Christopher Brianas and Debbie Potratz.

This research benefited from helpful insights and comments provided by several RAND colleagues, including Craig Bond, Lisa Harrington, Pete Schirmer, Harry Thie, and John Winkler; their thoughtful comments greatly improved this report. Sean Mann contributed greatly to the data quality analyses and file structuring. We also thank Barbara Bicksler for her contributions to making this study concise and consistent in its messaging.

Abbreviations

CCMD	combatant command
CJCS	Chairman of the Joint Chiefs of Staff
CJCSI	Chairman of the Joint Chiefs of Staff Instruction
DoD	Department of Defense
DoDI	Department of Defense Instruction
E-JDA	experience joint duty assignment
GNA	Goldwater-Nichols Department of Defense Reorganization Act
HFP	hostile fire pay
IDP	imminent danger pay
JCWS	Joint and Combined Warfighting School
JDAL	joint duty assignment list
JDAMIS	Joint Duty Assignment Management Information System
JIA	joint individual augmentation
JOM	joint officer management
JPME	joint professional military education
JPME-I	joint professional military education (Phase 1)
JPME-II	joint professional military education (Phase 2)
JQO	joint qualified officer
JQS	joint qualification system
JTF	joint task force
NDAA	National Defense Authorization Act
OSD	Office of the Secretary of Defense
PME	professional military education
S-JDA	standard joint duty assignment
SJS	senior joint school
SSS	senior service school

CHAPTER ONE

Introduction

The History of Joint Qualified Officers

With the passage of the Goldwater-Nichols Department of Defense Reorganization Act (GNA) of 1986,[1] the Department of Defense (DoD) began its transition from mostly independent military services to a more effective and capable joint organization. While the GNA instituted comprehensive changes in the organizational structure and functional authorities of DoD (e.g., military chain of command, reporting and advisory authorities, procurement guidelines, warfare doctrine development), a key personnel element focused on the career-long development of officers who were specifically educated and experienced in "joint matters." The goal was to increase the quality, stability, and experience of officers assigned to joint organizations—such as the Joint Staff or combatant commands (CCMDs)—which, in turn, would improve joint outcomes. To accomplish these objectives, the GNA sought reforms and modification centered around four elements of the officer management system:

1. joint professional military education (JPME) in accredited joint schools
2. a joint duty assignment list (JDAL) that provided experiential application of joint knowledge
3. designation of joint specialty officers for those who successfully completed the combination of an appropriate level of joint education and duty assignments
4. joint criteria and benchmarks associated with officer promotions.

Appreciating that the services retained control of officer assignment and promotion processes, the act mandated specific designation of jointly trained and experienced officers as a prerequisite for promotion to the general and flag officer ranks, minimum tour lengths for joint positions, and a reporting system that sought to ensure compliance and reward joint experience.

The fundamental elements for educating and managing joint officers are codified in Title 10 of the U.S. Code and further implemented via Department of Defense

---

[1] Public Law 99-433, Goldwater-Nichols Department of Defense Reorganization Act of 1986, October 1, 1986.

Instructions (DoDIs) and Chairman of the Joint Chiefs of Staff Instructions (CJCSIs).[2] Within the context of these instructions (and throughout this report), JPME and joint officer management (JOM) are considered separate functions under the broader umbrella of officer talent management. In fact, both the Office of the Secretary of Defense (OSD) and the Joint Staff have separate offices responsible for the unique functions of JOM and JPME. Over time, these separate offices have modified and updated the respective instructions to reflect both policy and operational considerations associated with and affecting officer education and career management.

In the 30-plus years since the GNA's implementation, many DoD entities, independent analytical organizations, and congressional committees have conducted a range of research initiatives and assessments.[3] Their findings have broadly included the following:

- *There is a tension between the needs of the services and the joint community for officer education, assignments, and career progression.* Joint commitments, for example, can be viewed as detrimental to an officer's career while service-specific education and assignments are often perceived to be more valuable to promotion. Officers are finding it increasingly challenging to complete required JPME, which is even more difficult when there are continuous operational requirements.
- *Nothing in law or policy specifies the sequencing of JPME, Phase II (JPME-II) and a joint duty assignment.* That being said, the Chairman of the Joint Chiefs of Staff (CJCS) stated in 2010 that there was benefit in education preceding a duty

---

[2] CJCSI 1800.01E, 2015a; CJCSI 1330.05A, *Joint Officer Management Program Procedures*, December 15, 2015b; DoDI 1300.19, 2018; United States Code, Title 10, Subtitle A, General Military Law, Part II, Personnel, Chapter 38, Joint Officer Management; United States Code, Title 10, Subtitle A, General Military Law, Part III, Training and Education, Chapter 107, Professional Military Education.

[3] U.S. House of Representatives, Committee on Armed Services, Subcommittee on Oversight and Investigations, *Another Crossroads? Professional Military Education Two Decades After the Goldwater-Nichols Act and the Skelton Panel*, Washington, D.C.: House Armed Services Committee, April 2010; Kristy Kamarck, *Goldwater-Nichols and the Evolution of Officer Joint Professional Military Education*, Washington, D.C.: Congressional Research Service, R44340, 2016; U.S. Government Accountability Office, *Actions Needed to Implement DoD Recommendations for Enhancing Leadership Development*, Washington, D.C.: U.S. Government Accountability Office, GAO-14-29, 2013; Linda Fenty, *The Joint Staff Officer Report*, Washington, D.C.: Joint Staff J7 / Joint Training Division, 2008; Clark A. Murdock, Michèle A. Flournoy, Kurt M. Campbell, Pierre A. Chao, Julianne Smith, Anne A. Witkowsky, and Christine E. Wormuth, *Beyond Goldwater-Nichols: U.S. Government and Defense Reform for a New Strategic Era—Phase 2 Report*, Washington, D.C.: Center for Strategic and International Studies, July 2005; Harry J. Thie, Margaret C. Harrell, Roland J. Yardley, Marian Oshiro, Holly Ann Potter, Peter Schirmer, and Nelson Lim, *Framing a Strategic Approach for Joint Officer Management*, Santa Monica, Calif.: RAND Corporation, MG-306-OSD, 2005; Booz Allen Hamilton, *Independent Study of Joint Officer Management and Joint Professional Military Education*, McLean, Va.: Booz Allen Hamilton, 2003; Ryan Shaw and Miriam Krieger, "Don't Leave Jointness to the Services: Preserving Joint Officer Development amid Goldwater-Nichols Reform," *War on the Rocks*, December 30, 2015.

assignment.[4] Despite this, officers have been assigned to joint positions without completing appropriate joint educational coursework in advance. This disconnect between JPME-II and joint duty assignments can become common practice, disregarding a fundamental purpose of JPME, which is proper preparation of officers for those assignments.

- *Because requisite JPME-II does not always precede joint assignments, officers may lack certain critical abilities necessary to perform their jobs effectively.*[5] Some operational joint commanders reportedly consider their joint officers lacking in certain critical abilities necessary to perform their jobs effectively. This often comes at a cost to combatant commanders not only as a performance decrement but also in the time and resources needed to complete JPME-II during the joint tour assignment.

In light of such findings, DoD has continued to reform and refine its JPME-II offerings, processes, and assessments through both policy and legislative changes. For example, such revisions have expanded the designated institutions eligible to provide JPME-II and allowed some portions of JPME-II to be completed via distance learning. Other changes have strengthened individual incentives by offering accredited master's degrees for both professional military education (PME) and JPME-II completion at all senior joint schools (SJSs), senior service schools (SSSs), and some intermediate service schools and allowing more flexibility in follow-on assignments to manage individual career paths and service-specific requirements. A revised joint qualification system (JQS) has been implemented that emphasizes joint experience as a pathway to joint qualification by establishing different levels of joint qualification.

Given the preponderance of such policy changes and enhancements over time, DoD needs to have valid methods, procedures, and data to establish and assess trends in achieving educational requirements and accomplishing joint assignments. Thus, the overall objective of this research is to quantify and assess the production of joint qualified officers (JQOs) to establish a baseline of JOM and JPME outcomes from which to assess historical trends. Such information does not currently exist and is not systematically reviewed for implications and practices that would have cross-service benefits. This report provides such historical trends for field grade officers (O-4 to O-6) in the active component over a ten-year time period.

---

[4] Chairman of the Joint Chiefs of Staff Memorandum CM-1081-10, *Joint Qualified Officer (Level III) Requirements*, June 8, 2010, p. 1, states, "I am convinced that the benefits of completing JPME-II prior to a joint duty assignment are a force multiplier for the Services and the gaining joint organization."

[5] Sheila Nataraj Kirby, Al Crego, Harry J. Thie, Margaret C. Harrell, Kimberly Curry Hall, and Michael S. Tseng, *Who Is "Joint"? New Evidence from the 2005 Joint Officer Management Census Survey*, Santa Monica, Calif.: RAND Corporation, TR-349-OSD, 2006, offers one of the most comprehensive reports on joint officers, their workload, supervision, preparations, and perceptions. In this census survey, almost 92 percent of officers in JDAL billets reported that "JPME-II is required or desired for the assignment," p. 88.

Joint Officer Data

To oversee the management and designation of joint officer education and qualifications, DoD created the Joint Duty Assignment Management Information System (JDAMIS), which is managed by the Defense Manpower Data Center and contains both current and historical data regarding officer joint qualifications for all services.[6] Over time, statutes and polices regarding joint education and officer management have expanded, both in terms of officers considered for joint qualification (e.g., reserve component officers, more junior officers, officers serving in civilian or military technician capacity) and the range of experiences considered as eligible for joint credit, as was previously discussed. The associated complexity and diversity of these changes has resulted in a patchwork of modifications and updates to JDAMIS.

Unfortunately, JDAMIS has never been a DoD system of record, nor does the system have dedicated funding for maintenance and upgrades.[7] Therefore, the informal program has been inconsistently executed over many years. There is no overarching strategy or system architecture to guide and prioritize efforts to maintain, sustain, or enhance the collective system and its essential data specification, much less prepare needed system documentation. As a result, a number of limitations in using the data have been documented by the Joint Staff.[8] While efforts are underway to fully update and modernize the joint officer management and education system, analytical efforts that rely solely on JDAMIS data are somewhat hindered, as is detailed in the next section.

Data Quality and Analytical Limits

To assess the magnitude of these documented JDAMIS data deficiencies, our initial research efforts focused on a range of data quality analyses centered on variables involved in the development of JQOs. This included efforts to quantify and display the sequence of events that resulted in the designation of a JQO—an individual's history and source of joint educational attainment, as well as the timing, duration, and successful completion of a joint assignment or assignments. To the extent possible, we conducted quality control analysis seeking to ensure that data agreed with information provided by other official sources (e.g., congressional or OSD reports). However, even

---

[6]   CJCSI 1330.05A, 2015b; Joint Staff J1, Directorate for Manpower and Personnel / Joint Officer Management Office, *Joint Chiefs of Staff Joint Duty Assignment Management Information System, Volume 1—Files*, Washington, D.C.: Joint Staff J1, undated.

[7]   Charles H. Porter, Kory Fierstine, S. Craig Goodwyn, and David Gregory, *Joint Officer Management Modernization Analysis of Alternatives (AoA)*, Washington, D.C.: Center for Naval Analyses, 2017.

[8]   Joint Staff J1, Directorate for Manpower and Personnel, *Problem Statement: Joint Officer Management (JOM) Modernization, Version 2.5*, Washington, D.C.: Joint Staff J1, August 7, 2014.

such authoritative or official sources have occasionally been called into question based on JDAMIS data issues:

> In the fall of 2016, large data errors related to Joint Duty Assignment List size and billet fill rates were identified by the Joint Staff and Services in the draft report. Efforts by the Defense Management [sic: Manpower] Data Center to resolve these programming errors were recently completed. However, continuing JDAMIS system limitations prevent Joint Staff validation of the accuracy of all data.[9]

Accordingly, to the extent possible, we sought to conduct other multimethod, multi-source analyses to confirm that data were internally consistent (e.g., that showed reasonable timing and occurrence of events) and replicated data from other data sets (e.g., officer master file). We highlight in our report where we make any modifications, deletions, or adjustments to data when such inconsistencies were observed.

Based on these quality assessments, we narrowed the scope of our analysis to active component, Level III JQOs in grades O-4 to O-6 for the period FY 2008 to FY 2017. Our rationale is as follows:

- *The last ten fiscal years of available data (FY 2008 to FY 2017).* We noted anomalies with JDAMIS information over time. Older data tended to have greater problems. Specifically, it appears that annual totals for the number of individuals appointed as JQOs were aggregated into a single year, FY 2006, with zero individuals being appointed during FY 2004 or FY 2005. Similarly, there was a considerable downward spike in JQO designations in FY 2007 that could not be explained despite the significant number of operational deployments during that time frame. These discrepancies also led to inconsistent findings for the total inventory of JQOs in those corresponding years.
- *JQOs at Level III.*[10] Level II and Level IV JQOs are the beginning and ending points for the systematic career-long development process of officers in joint matters. Level II officers tend to be more junior service members who have successfully completed JPME Phase I (JPME-I) coursework and a limited amount of joint tour experience. Level IV corresponds to general and flag officers who have accomplished a more rigorous and extensive battery of education (the Capstone program) and joint assignments. We found Level II data to be somewhat less consistent than Level III data over a range of variables and time periods. Information

---

[9]   Joint Staff J1, Directorate for Manpower and Personnel, *Fiscal Year 2016 Joint Officer Management Annual Report*, Washington, D.C.: Joint Staff J1, April 3, 2017.

[10]   From this point forth in our report, we use the abbreviation JQO to refer specifically and uniquely to a JQO Level III. As noted earlier, we acknowledge that there are Level II and Level IV JQOs, but for data quality concerns and other issues, we have excluded those levels from our analytical consideration.

for Level IV officers was limited in annual sample sizes across services and was determined to best be assessed via more qualitative methods.

- *Active component officers.* While JDAMIS is intended to focus on the full spectrum of military officers (in the active and reserve components), our quality analysis showed that only the active component data were generally consistent with other data sources and verification means. It appears that data associated with reserve component personnel who transition between part-time and full-time statuses were inconsistently coded over time.
- *Officers in the grades of O-4 to O-6.* As a matter of policy, officers of the grade O-3 and below (lieutenants in the Navy and captains in all other services) are considered too junior and therefore are not eligible for JQO designation.

Data constraints also did not allow us to consider the demand associated with JQOs as would be specified in the JDAL.[11] We also did not report trends for demographic or breakout groups that were composed of five or fewer individuals. In such cases, tables that include data categories with small cell entries may not consistently sum to expected totals.

The Study Approach

Based on the data set described in the previous section—field grade active-duty officers who were designated as Level III JQOs from FY 2008 to FY 2017—we conducted assessments based on the following:

- *JQO inventory.* We analyzed the inventory of JQOs on an annual basis, examining trends and notable distinctions by policy-relevant categories—service, grade, and occupational code. Similarly, we examined the annual number of JQO appointees for the same categories. We calculated both absolute numbers of officers and the respective percentage of such officers within each service to examine differences both within and across services.
- *Joint education and experience.* Based on our understanding of the overall supply of JQOs, we explored the respective intermediate components that are required for JQO designation—graduating JPME-II and accomplishing joint experience through an appropriate duty assignment. With regard to joint education, we examined the historical trends for graduates from JPME-II granting institutions, as well as the success rate of various institutions in generating JQOs after a fixed period of time. With regard to joint experience, we considered the two primary

---

[11] The JDAL is a list of positions continuously validated by the Joint Staff such that an officer gains significant experience in joint matters.

paths to achieving joint experience—a standard joint duty assignment (S-JDA) and an experience joint duty assignment (E-JDA). This involved how these paths evolved over time, as well as differences in how the services used such options.

- *Sequencing of education and experience.* Third, we examined the intersection of accomplishing joint education and joint experience—both the sequencing of these two elements (whether education was completed prior to, during, or after the duty assignment) and the time duration between JPME-II graduation and JQO accomplishment. To the extent that data were available, we related short intervals to waivers or unique officer assignment circumstances.
- *Case studies.* We explored a case study of Army brigadier generals as of 2018 to gain a better understanding of how recent senior military leaders accomplished both of these joint qualifying elements, and a second case study of O-5s to examine the relationship between JQO designations and promotion experiences.

As context for the data analyses, we compiled and analyzed relevant JPME-II and joint duty assignment statutes and current DoD, Joint Staff, and military department policies related to joint education and assignments—summarizing the historical, current, and future relevance of these statutes and policies. We also reviewed previous studies of JPME—specifically, those focused on the intersection of JPME-II processes and follow-on joint assignments (but not studies focused on CCMD requirements, joint curriculum determination and its revision, or faculty-student issues at joint educational institutions).

Finally, we used the trend analysis and other results to engage the JOM and JPME offices of the services and Joint Staff to gain a historical context and to appreciate possible factors that may have contributed to variance. The purpose of these interactions was to better understand the offices' perceptions on the validity of the data presented, gain their historical recollections of policy and operational events that could have affected JQO findings, understand their thoughts on the implications of the JQO findings, and identify potential JPME-JOM practices that they perceived to have been effective or could benefit others. Such considerations may serve as the basis for further evaluating policy outcomes and/or examining the need for additional policy refinements. As it generally takes considerable time for the effects of policy changes to be realized, these presentations serve as a baseline against which to assess change, impact, and direction of effects.

The Organization of the Report

Our report is organized around two primary areas: governing policies, and trends in developing JQOs. In Chapter Two we detail the evolving policies that have governed the development of JQOs. In Chapters Three through Five we present and analyze trends over the last ten years for the various elements required to produce JQOs—covering historical trends in JQO inventory, accomplishment of joint education and experience, sequencing of education and experience, and the use of waivers. Chapter Six explores two case studies to illustrate experiences of JQOs in senior grades. In Chapter Seven we discuss the implications of these trends for both policy and operational organizations associated with either JOM or JPME.

CHAPTER TWO

Achieving Designation as a Joint Qualified Officer

The process for joint qualification has evolved from its origins in the GNA. As context for understanding trends in the development of JQOs that will be discussed in the remainder of this report, this section provides an overview of the current elements involved in the joint qualification process, including defense policy governing joint qualification and changes in JOM and JPME-II policies and statutes. An appreciation of the changes in the system that have taken place over time is useful for interpreting our analytical findings.

Defense Policy Governing Joint Qualification

In order to enhance joint warfighting capability and lethality, DoD has established new policies and modified existing ones that designate officers as joint qualified at progressive levels of accomplishment. These joint qualification levels (II, III, and IV) reflect achievement of increasingly higher criteria associated with education and duty assignments over the course of an officer's career.[1]

Since the time of GNA implementation, the traditional JQO designation path involved the completion of the JPME-II program at a senior joint educational institution and a tour of duty in a JDAL position that was at least 36 months long. Over time, the services and individual officers found this process rigorous and not reflective of the dynamic environment in which the joint forces operated. During Operations Enduring Freedom and Iraqi Freedom, joint operations had transformed considerably with joint task force (JTF) employment concepts and other joint organizational designs that involved interagency, intergovernmental, and multinational participants to include nongovernmental partners. As configured at that time, the joint qualification process did not recognize such experiences as joint, nor were they considered to be of sufficient duration (36 months or greater). But the demands in which joint forces were then operating—multiple deployments, significant joint contributions provided

---

[1] Level I, which focused on precommissioning and junior officers, was dropped with the recent update of DoDI 1300.19, 2018.

by reserve component forces, and limited time at the home station for nondeployment considerations—provided justification for modifying the joint qualification process.

In response to these considerations, Congress authorized DoD in the FY 2007 National Defense Authorization Act (NDAA) to establish a new JQS with greater fidelity in assessing the joint capabilities of officers:

> The Secretary of Defense shall establish different levels of joint qualification, as well as the criteria for qualification at each level. Such levels of joint qualification shall be established by the Secretary with the advice of the Chairman of the Joint Chiefs of Staff. Each level shall, as a minimum, have both joint education criteria and joint experience criteria. The purpose of establishing such qualification levels is to ensure a systematic, progressive, career-long development of officers in joint matters and to ensure that officers serving as general and flag officers have the requisite experience and education to be highly proficient in joint matters.[2]

Therefore, in addition to the traditional path for designating an officer as joint qualified (now referred to as S-JDA), DoD implemented a complementary points-based path within the JQS. This new dimension of the system recognized and valued a range of experiences based on shorter-duration operational assignments, joint training, other education contributing to expertise in joint matters, participation in exercises, and self-development learning activities. This new "experienced-based" track was named E-JDA. The analytical underpinnings for the design and development of E-JDA stemmed from analysis focused on identifying the characteristics associated with joint billets. This work formed a basis for policymakers to determine how to assign joint duty credit and thereby which positions were good candidates for the JDAL.[3]

Accomplishing either of these tracks—S-JDAs or E-JDAs—in combination with the appropriate level of joint education resulted in an individual being designated as joint qualified at Level II or Level III. Level III is also known as JQO. The S-JDA approach is considered the primary method for attaining JQO Level III qualification. With the implementation of the JQS, all former joint specialty officers—so designated in prior years—were reclassified as JQOs and the joint specialty officer characterization was dropped.

Table 2.1 provides further details for understanding the dual paths to joint qualification (Levels II and III) and the associated point thresholds for achieving qualification under E-JDA. The thresholds provided in this figure are based on the most recent

---

[2]   U.S. Congress, 109th Cong., 2nd Sess., *John Warner National Defense Authorization Act for Fiscal Year 2007: Conference Report to Accompany H.R. 5122*, Washington, D.C.: U.S. Government Printing Office, Report 109-702, 2006.

[3]   Margaret C. Harrell, Harry J. Thie, Sheila Nataraj Kirby, Al Crego, Danielle M. Varda, and Thomas Sullivan, *A Strategic Approach to Joint Officer Management: Analysis and Modeling Results*, Santa Monica, Calif.: RAND Corporation, MG-886-OSD, 2009, served as the basis and analytical underpinnings for OSD developing the JQS.

Table 2.1
Joint Qualification System Designation Elements

Typical Officer Level	Joint Education	Joint Experience			Administrative Classification	JQO Level	Designating Authority	Objective Outcome
		S-JDA	or	E-JDA				
O3–O4	Intermediate JPME-I	Full joint duty credit (at least 24 months, with at least 12 months as O4 or higher)[a]		12 total points Joint duty or experience (6 min pts) Discretionary (6 max pts)	After JPME and JDA completion: • Service nomination • Service review • Approval • Designation	Level II	Secretary of military department	Career-long development of officers in joint matters
O5–O6	Senior JPME-II	Full joint duty credit (at least 24 months, with at least 12 months as O4 or higher)[a]		24 total points (12 beyond Level II) Joint duty (≥12 months) and experience (18 min pts) Discretionary (6 max pts)	After JPME and JDA completion: • Service nomination • Joint staff and OSD review • Approval • Designation	Level III JQO	Under Secretary of Defense for Personnel and Readiness	

SOURCE: DoDI 1300.19, 2018.

[a] Despite a minimum of 24 months, tour assignments are made on basis of a full tour of 36 months. Tour length waivers (<22 months) are discouraged and tend to be the exception. Time in position as O4 or higher reflects the recency requirement of joint experience needed as a field grade officer.

update of DoDI 1300.19. Prior to this update, many of the threshold requirements were higher.

We focus first on achieving joint experience via an S-JDA—this path through which the majority of officers will complete a joint duty assignment. A successful S-JDA requires the officer to be selected for and serve in a position on the JDAL for a standard tour length of at least 24 months.[4] There are waivers to this tour length requirement, though they are discouraged and tend to be the exception. Officers must be in grades O-3 to O-6. There is a recency requirement: a minimum of 12 months in a JDAL position must come from joint experience earned in the pay grade of O-4 or higher. Accomplishing these requirements results in full joint duty credit, and this completion satisfies the joint experience requirement for designation as both Level II and III joint qualified.

Conversely, an officer can proceed with an E-JDA that is based on accumulating sufficient points to achieve joint experience equivalent to a full joint duty credit assignment. Qualification points are awarded for both experience and discretionary activities.

Joint experience points can be received for (1) serving in a Joint Staff-approved non-JDAL assignment that demonstrates an officer's mastery in joint matters, or (2) serving partial time in a JDAL position (less than 24 months results in accrued joint duty assignment credit; unless a tour length waiver is given). Points are calculated based on the duration (months) of service and intensity associated with the assignment. The intensity factor multiplied by the duration of the assignment enters into the calculation of experiential points and is determined based on the officer's receipt of hostile fire pay (HFP) or imminent danger pay (IDP). Receiving this stipend results in a multiplier of two; not receiving it is a multiplier of one. Any product of duration and intensity that equals or exceeds 24 is consider the equivalent of a full joint tour of duty for the S-JDA.

Prior to an officer receiving credit for this joint experience, he or she must submit appropriate documentation of an assignment within 12 months of completion to the Joint Staff for adjudication (often referred to as administrative classification). After screening by the officer's respective service, the Joint Staff will validate both the duration and intensity determinations that are the basis for the points calculation. Looking back to Table 2.1, an officer must receive at least six experience points to be considered for Level II joint qualification and at least 18 to be considered for Level III joint quali-

---

[4] For this revision of joint tour duration, the services argued that their respective command assignments typically did not exceed 24 months and that the number of waivers for tour length curtailment, in effect, resulted in joint assignments being 24 months or less. Conversely, Kirby, Crego, Thie, Harrell, Hall, and Tseng, 2006, reported that respondents of the 2005 census survey thought that the optimal length of time for joint tours of duty was 36 months. On average, officers in JDAL billets reported that it took about five months to become comfortable operating in a joint environment. There was no difference in responses by whether individuals had received JPME-II credit. Higher-ranked officers appeared to become comfortable in billet assignments more quickly than other officers.

fication (12 more points than what was received previously at Level II). Within limits, discretionary points may substitute for these experience points.

The E-JDA process also recognizes that officers may also gain experience in joint matters through participation in activities such as joint training and education (other than JPME) and joint exercises—and these experiences can contribute to joint qualification through assignment of discretionary points. Yet an officer cannot earn joint qualification only through such activities. Therefore, discretionary points are capped at a maximum of six (across both joint qualification levels), as is shown in Table 2.1.

DoDI 1300.19 notes that the Joint Staff will establish a process to certify joint individual training courses that contribute to an officer's expertise in joint matters and assign qualification points based on course content and duration. On a quarterly basis, the Joint Staff J7 publishes the Joint Qualification Report, which details these courses, their content areas, the method of administration (distributed, institutional, or blended), contact hours, points, and certification date.[5] Likewise, the Joint Staff will identify, maintain, and publish an annual list of joint exercises that qualify for joint qualification points. Officers who are key participants, planners, or leaders in such documented exercises may receive up to one point for such joint exercise roles.

The final component of JQO level determination is graduation from an accredited institution offering JPME-I or JPME-II. Table 2.2 lists these institutions for both the intermediate (Phase I) and senior (Phase II) levels of joint education. Although a number of international military colleges also approved for JPME-I equivalence, relatively few U.S. officers attend and graduate from these alternative programs.[6]

Finally, for an officer to be designated as Level III qualified, a range of administrative reviews and decisions must be completed. First, a military service must nominate the officer for joint qualification. Even with all joint education, experience, and quality criteria satisfied, not all service members are immediately nominated for joint qualification, sometimes due to the needs of the service. Once nominated, the member's package is thoroughly reviewed and vetted by the Joint Staff and then similarly by the Office of the Secretary of Defense. Assuming these requirements are satisfied, the appropriate designating authority signs off—the military service secretary or the Under Secretary of Defense for Personnel and Readiness. At this point the Joint Staff will ensure that the appropriate qualification level is updated in JDAMIS.

Permeating this entire process of defining the required elements for joint qualification is the question of what constitutes "joint matters." Joint matters is codified in law and based on joint doctrine.[7] It is the basis for defining and assessing joint edu-

---

[5] Joint Staff J7, Joint Force Development, *Joint Qualification Report, Fiscal Year 2018, 3rd Quarter*, Washington, D.C.: Joint Staff J1, June 30, 2018.

[6] Chairman of the Joint Chiefs of Staff Memorandum CM-1084-14, *Program for Joint Professional Military Education Phase I Equivalent Credit*, June 27, 2014.

[7] Definitions shown here are drawn from United States Code, Title 10, Chapter 38, §668, and DoDI, 2018.

Table 2.2
Accredited Institutions Offering JPME

Institutions	Service	Joint
Intermediate Education—JPME-I	Air Command and Staff College Army Command and General Staff College College of Naval Command and Staff Marine Corps Command and Staff College (With CJCS prior approval, JPME-I sequencing can be waivered (via a direct entry waiver) so that it is achieved concurrently with JPME-II, though this is exceptionally rare)	Joint and Combined Warfighting School (JCWS) National Intelligence University
Senior Education—JPME-II	Air War College Army War College College of Naval Warfare Marine Corps War College	National War College Dwight D. Eisenhower School for National Security and Resource Security JCWS and JCWS-Hybrid Joint and Combined Staff Officer School Joint Advanced Warfighting School College of International Security Affairs School of Information Warfare and Strategy

SOURCE: CJCSI 1800-01E, 2015a.

cation, JDAL positions, and individual joint experiences. The statutory definition of joint matters provides the two critical circumstances for compliance:

- *What You Do:* Matters related to development or achievement of strategic objectives through synchronization, coordination, and organization of integrated forces in operations conducted across domains such as land, sea, or air; in space; or in an information environment, including matters related to
  a. national military strategy; strategic planning and contingency planning; command and control, intelligence, fires, movement and maneuver, protection, or sustainment of operations under unified command
  b. national security planning with other U.S. departments and agencies
  c. combined operations with military forces of allied nations
  d. acquisition matters conducted by service members and covered under Chapter 87 of U.S. Code, Title 10, involved in developing, testing, contracting, producing, or fielding of multiservice programs or systems.

- *Who You Do It With:* Integrated forces refers to military forces that are involved in achieving unified action with participants from
  a. more than one military department, or
  b. a military department and one or more of the following:
      i.   other departments and agencies of the United States
      ii.   military forces or agencies of other countries
      iii. nongovernmental persons or entities.

Since the introduction of the GNA, the definition of joint matters has expanded to include broader specifications of joint activities (e.g., command and control, intelligence, fires, movement and maneuver, protection, or sustainment), as well as inclusion of specific credence given to acquisition matters. A portion of the preliminary justification and eventual revision of this definitional change was the result of the census survey of joint officers undertaken by Sheila Nataraj Kirby and colleagues in which they further explored the dimension of jointness.[8] Their research defined "highly joint" tasks as (1) providing strategic direction and integration; (2) developing/assessing joint policies; (3) developing/assessing joint doctrine; and (4) fostering multinational, interagency, alliance, or regional relations. The survey showed that 80 percent of officers assigned to JDAL billets performed one or more "highly joint" tasks—results that were considerably higher than officers assigned to non-JDAL billets.

Changes in Joint Officer Management and JPME-II Policies and Statutes

Several factors affect the interpretation of our analytical findings and JOM and JPME trends, including policy and statute changes that have occurred over time, differences in services' execution of these policies, and operational considerations. A history and timeline for such changes is presented in Table 2.3.

The GNA was passed in 1986 and established the basic joint talent management parameters as a combination of specific JOM and JPME-II criteria. Previously we discussed the respective elements of the GNA and its associated enforcement metrics and reports. Between 1987 and 1989, Representative Ike Skelton chaired a House of Representatives panel to specifically examine GNA implementation relative to military education. The subsequent report produced a range of recommendations that were reflected in the FY 1990 and FY 1991 NDAAs.[9] Most significantly, the Skelton Panel recommended a two-phase education process. JPME-I was intended to be

---

[8] Kirby, Crego, Thie, Harrell, Hall, and Tseng, 2006.

[9] U.S. House of Representatives, Committee on Armed Services, *Report of the Panel on Military Education of the One Hundredth Congress*, Washington, D.C.: U.S. Government Printing Office, April 21, 1989.

Table 2.3
Timeline for Joint Officer Management and JPME-II Policy and Statute Changes

Source	Policy/Statute Changes
1986 GNA	• JPME + JDAL assignment = joint specialty officer designation • General or flag officer promotions require joint experience
1989 Skelton Panel	• Recommends creation of 2-phase curriculum; Phase II, 3+ months • Recommends establishing learning objectives and standards • Recommends accrediting institutions, faculty-staff ratios
FY 1994 NDAA	• Endorses separation of PME and JPME • Allows joint duty assignment as second versus first assignment • Confers master of science degrees in national security
FY 2002 NDAA	• Requires independent JOM/JPME study • Requires strategic JOM reform approach
FY 2005 NDAA	• Requires new strategic plan for JPME • Defines curricular content and requirements
FY 2007 NDAA	• Allows DoD to establish the JQS • Allows Service Schools to teach JPME-II • Removes JPME-I & II prior to assignment
FY 2012 NDAA	• Conducts pilot program (5 years) • Allows for distributed (not in-residence) JPME-II • Recommends initially at the Joint Special Operations University and CENTCOM
FY 2015 NDAA	• JPME-II can be met with a senior-level service course of at least 10 months
2015, CJCSI 1330.05A	• Single-phase JPME withdrawn
2015, CJCSI 1800.01E	• Establishes desired leader attributes • Values advanced distributed learning • Updates learning areas, objectives
FY 2016 NDAA	• Acquisition added to joint matters definition • Allows joint assignments to be 2 years or less
2018, DoDI 1300.19	• Reduces joint assignments to no less than 2 years • Reduces JQO qualification points • Reduces exercise discretionary points • Expands joint matters definition

taught in the service colleges, with a sequential JPME-II to be taught at the Armed Forces Staff College (which later became the Joint Forces Staff College). Similarly, the Skelton Report established critical learning objectives and standards for each joint education level, faculty standards and staffing ratios, and the foundations for academic accreditation.

In the FY 1994 NDAA, Congress confirmed the value of separating military education institutions providing PME from joint schools focused on JPME. It also allowed greater flexibility in joint duty assignments so that JPME-II graduates could serve in a joint duty assignment as their second (rather than first) assignment after completing their JPME. The NDAA also provided greater incentive for quality officers to seek and desire joint education as a result of conferring a master's degree in national security strategy and national resource strategy on JPME-II graduation.

Over the next few years, both legislative and policy actions focused on establishing the strategic framework for JOM and JPME-II. Across several NDAAs, Congress called for an independent study of the interaction of JOM and JPME-II. This work was completed in 2003.[10] Subsequently, Congress asked RAND to develop a strategic approach for reforming the JOM system.[11] The net result of these studies was captured in the NDAA for FY 2005 by adding Capstone JPME requirements for general and flag officers, defining in greater detail the curriculum content for JPME-II, requiring the sequential accomplishment of JPME-I and JPME-II (to be instituted by FY 2010), and specifying student and faculty ratios across services for JPME-II institutions.

As a result of OSD submitting the JPME strategic plan, Congress reinforced its commitment to joint experience in the FY 2007 NDAA by allowing DoD to establish a JQS—a points-based system allowing accumulation of credits comparable with joint duty assignments.[12] (The JQS was discussed in greater detail in an earlier section of this report.) This legislation also relaxed the JPME requirement that officers complete both Phases I and II prior to receiving a joint duty assignment. Joint education institutions were also consolidated under the National Defense University—to include the Dwight D. Eisenhower School for National Security and Resource Security (formerly the Industrial College of the Armed Forces), the Joint Forces Staff College, and the National War College.

In 2010 a subcommittee of the House Committee on Armed Services reported on its review of service and JPME in the context of complex and evolving national security challenges.[13] The subcommittee found a number of system issues, institutional issues, and issues for further study. One of its most significant findings was that the completion of and demand for JPME appears to be more closely tied to promotion potential than to developing required competencies to serve in joint duty assignments.

Between FY 2008 and FY 2016, the NDAAs made minimal references to JPME:

- The FY 2010 NDAA made slight refinement of "integrated military forces" within the definition of joint matters to explicitly include more than one military department or other specifications of participants.

---

[10] Booz Allen Hamilton, 2003.

[11] Thie, Harrell, Yardley, Oshiro, Potter, Schirmer, and Lim, 2005.

[12] Harrell, Thie, Kirby, Crego, Varda, and Sullivan, 2009, served as the basis and analytical underpinnings for developing the JQS.

[13] U.S. House of Representatives, Committee on Armed Services, Subcommittee on Oversight and Investigations, 2010.

- The FY 2012 NDAA authorized a pilot study of conducting JPME-II at a satellite location. While formally considered "nonresidential" instruction because it was not conducted at a joint institution or SSS accredited for JPME-II, this pilot program was an exact content replica of the ten-week JCWS program. The pilot was conducted through the Joint Special Operations University for the joint officers resident at the U.S. Central Command and the U.S. Special Operations Command.
- The FY 2015 NDAA allowed Secretary of Defense–certified senior military service schools to award JPME-II credit for instructional programs that were of at least ten months.
- To address important issues in the field of acquisition and its subspecialties, the FY 2016 NDAA broadened the definition of joint matters to include joint duty credit for acquisition-related positions.

OSD and Joint Staff policies—articulated in and distributed via formal instructions—have tracked the changes that occurred in legislative authorizations. The most recent and updated version of these instructions is DoDI 1300.19, which was the result of considerable consultation and negotiation among the military services and the joint community: CCMDs, the Joint Staff, OSD, and defense agencies. The net result was reduction in effective time required for a full joint duty credit assignment to no less than two years. Despite this reduction, the intent is for the services to make assignments based on three-year tours. A compromise also involved the "clock" for any tour actually stopping for an individual who had not completed JPME-II when it was determined that the officer needed to return to the JCWS (ten weeks) to complete this requirement to satisfactorily perform his or her joint duties. Given these revisions to minimum tour lengths, comparable reductions were made to the point threshold for JQO qualification levels; this included lowering the number of discretionary points awarded for completion of either joint exercise roles or selected joint education courses. DoDI 1300.19 also implemented the addition of the acquisition perspective to the definition of joint matters.

CJCSI 1330.05A and CJCSI 1800.01E are currently being revised to align with the changes made in the newly published DoDI 1300.19. Prior revisions of both the JOM and JPME CJCSIs involved content upgrades defining desired leader attributes that were drivers to content revisions for JPME institutions, an acknowledgment of distributed learning as a current acceptable means of delivering education, and other updates to learning areas and objectives.

CHAPTER THREE

Historical Inventories of Joint Qualified Officers

As was discussed in Chapter Two, laws and policies determine the mechanisms through which officers become JQOs, but military service preferences influence the timing and sequencing. As we will illustrate in this chapter, the military services emphasize the joint tour component at different phases of an officer's career. Joint education appears to be largely disconnected from the joint tour in many instances, but stark differences among the services are evident in both the venue for JPME-II and the timing in the career. When combining the two ingredients of a JQO—the joint tour and joint education—differences among the services in timing of these events are also evident and vary with regard to when an individual "should" achieve JQO designation.

To guide the presentation of the JQO results as we present a large amount of data in the next several chapters, Table 3.1 details an organizational concept that characterizes the general question being addressed, the topics that help to answer the question, and the detailed considerations that are addressed for each topic area. We begin in this chapter by examining the historical inventories of JQOs. Chapter Four contains our analysis of officer experiences in accomplishing joint education and assignment requirements. Chapter Five presents our analysis of the sequencing of education and experience and the usage of waivers, and Chapter Six contains two case studies that explore typical paths for successful senior leaders.

To gain a picture of JQO supply, we examined trends in total inventory and annual production (i.e., newly appointed JQOs during the course of a given fiscal year).[1] Total inventories are more stable over time in that they reflect moving averages of the annual production numbers. For each of these trends, we examined a number of subcategories to identify and highlight important trend differences. These categories included time (fiscal year), service, grade, occupational category (tactical operations versus nontactical operations), JPME-II granting institution, type of joint experience (S-JDA versus E-JDA), and policy-relevant combinations of these variables that have sufficient sample sizes.

---

[1]   The time dimension associated with all trend analyses and findings is the time at which an officer achieved his or her JQO designation.

Table 3.1
Organization of Joint Qualified Officer Trends

Question	Topic	Considerations
What are the historical inventories of JQOs?	• Examining JQO inventories	• Cumulative inventory and annual appointees • Numbers and percentages • Variance by policy-relevant variables
How does an officer become a JQO?	• Accomplishing educational requirements	• Graduates by JPME institutions • JPME institutions that produced JQOs • Variance by policy-relevant variables
	• Accomplishing experience requirements	• Joint duty assignment path differences • Variance by policy-relevant variables
	• Sequencing of education and experience	• Before, during, and after sequences • Time between JPME graduation and JQO designation • Variance by policy-relevant variables
	• Considering waiver usage	• Tour length curtailment waivers only • Variance by policy-relevant variables
What are typical paths for successful senior leaders?	• Case study of Army brigadier generals • Contrast of O-5 promotions to O-6 based on JQO designation	• Educational experiences • Experiential paths • Variance by policy-relevant variables

We looked at both the number of JQOs and percentages (calculated based on the total number of individuals within the actual category or combination of categories examined). Examining the number of JQOs allows for absolute comparisons, while examination of percentages allows for relative or normalized comparisons. Numbers are more meaningful in a demand situation in which the interest is in how many JQOs were produced and whether that number was sufficient. Conversely, percentages are more interesting when making comparisons across groups (e.g., services) or trying to control for changes over time in external factors (e.g., variances in service end strength).

We will now highlight specific results and discuss their implications within the context of JOM and JPME-II, both within the joint community and for the services.

Trends by Service

Figures 3.1 and 3.2 present the number and percentage, respectively, for JQO inventory of active component field grade officers within each service across the last ten fiscal years. Based on these figures, the overall inventory trends are:

Figure 3.1
Field Grade Officer Joint Qualified Officer Inventory, by Service and Fiscal Year—Number

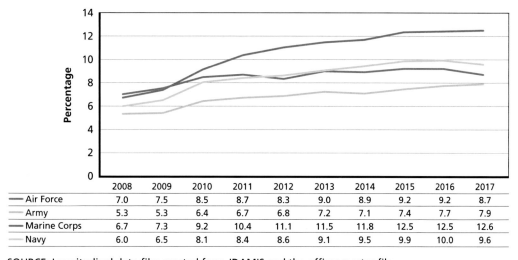

	2008	2009	2010	2011	2012	2013	2014	2015	2016	2017
—— Air Force	1,935	2,082	2,400	2,423	2,332	2,477	2,343	2,334	2,380	2,291
—— Army	1,526	1,585	1,960	2,120	2,180	2,321	2,218	2,226	2,220	2,202
—— Marine Corps	421	463	587	681	723	727	762	787	798	803
—— Navy	1,200	1,339	1,672	1,797	1,799	1,902	1,994	2,029	2,031	1,962

SOURCE: Longitudinal data files created from JDAMIS and the officer master file.

Figure 3.2
Field Grade Officer Joint Qualified Officer Inventory, by Service and Fiscal Year—Percentage

	2008	2009	2010	2011	2012	2013	2014	2015	2016	2017
—— Air Force	7.0	7.5	8.5	8.7	8.3	9.0	8.9	9.2	9.2	8.7
—— Army	5.3	5.3	6.4	6.7	6.8	7.2	7.1	7.4	7.7	7.9
—— Marine Corps	6.7	7.3	9.2	10.4	11.1	11.5	11.8	12.5	12.5	12.6
—— Navy	6.0	6.5	8.1	8.4	8.6	9.1	9.5	9.9	10.0	9.6

SOURCE: Longitudinal data files created from JDAMIS and the officer master file.

- Over the last ten fiscal years, JQO inventories of field grade active component officers have increased considerably—from about 5,100 to around 7,300 officers. While historically the number and duration of operational deployments were thought to adversely affect (or least appreciably delay) JQO production, with the advent of JQS, the JQO inventory has increased considerably due to experiential joint duty assignments resulting from combat duty. (We will examine E-JDA versus S-JDA differences in a later section.)

- From 2014 to 2017, the number of JQOs in inventory for each service are stable for all services except the Marine Corps, which achieved growth in all years.
- The Air Force has consistently had greater numbers of JQOs than the other services. Over the last four years, numbers in the Air Force inventory have constantly shown it to have about 250 more JQOs than the Army and about 500 more than the Navy.
- The greatest increases in inventory occurred in FY 2010 for all services. This year reflects the "grandfathering" enactment of a significant JOM policy: all officers were given until the end of FY 2010 to submit E-JDA applications for any assignment that had been completed more than one year earlier. After the 2010 cutoff date, all E-JDA submissions would be judged against the recency standard of experience within one year of completion.
- Compared to the other services, the Marine Corps consistently has a higher percentage of active component field grade officers who are JQOs, at 12.5 percent in FY 2017. The Army has shown consistent increases in these percentages over the last ten years. Inventories in both the Air Force and Navy have been relatively stable over the last five years, hovering around 9–10 percent (Figure 3.2).

Figures 3.3 and 3.4 show the number and percentage, respectively, for JQO inventory of active component field grade officers who were appointed as JQOs in each year. The following trends are evident:

- As with the inventory levels shown in the previous figures, the spike in FY 2010 JQO appointees reflects the onetime grandfathering of officers taking appropriate advantage of a change in JOM policy on receiving credit for recency of joint experience.
- In total, the number of active component field grade officers who were appointed as JQOs declined considerably in 2017, by over 250 in total across all the military services. The greatest decline was experienced by the Air Force, but all services showed a noticeable drop.
- Over time, the Air Force and the Army have shown the greatest variance both in terms of decreases and increases in annually appointed JQOs. It is not evident if the recent declines in appointees are a noticeable trend or just a reflection of considerable annual variance.
- The 2017 decline in officers appointed as JQOs is also reflected in the percentage metrics (Figure 3.4). Both the Air Force and Marine Corps appointees showed about a 0.5 percent decline in their respective officer corps compared with their respective service averages.

Figure 3.3
Field Grade Officers Appointed as Joint Qualified Officers, by Service and Fiscal Year—
Number

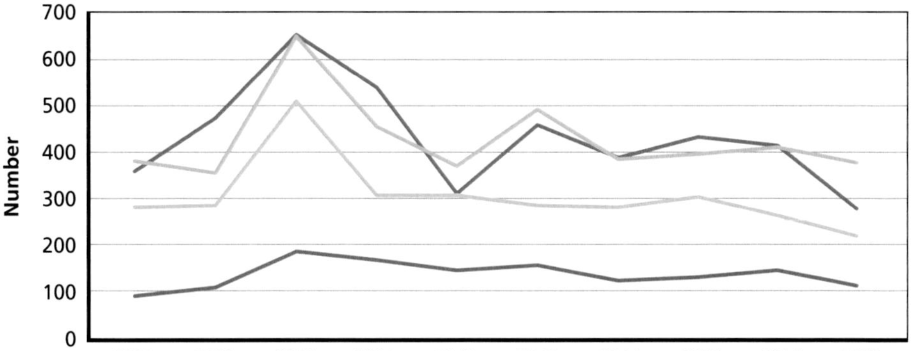

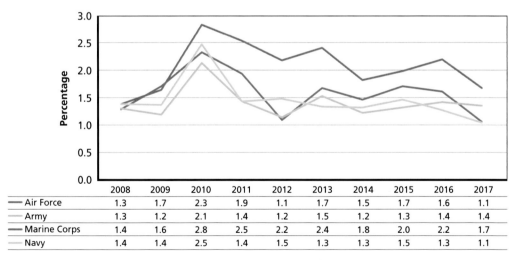

	2008	2009	2010	2011	2012	2013	2014	2015	2016	2017
Air Force	357	474	657	540	309	461	387	432	416	278
Army	380	354	655	454	368	492	386	397	411	376
Marine Corps	87	104	181	165	141	151	118	125	140	107
Navy	280	282	511	308	308	282	280	301	260	216

SOURCE: Longitudinal data files created from JDAMIS and the officer master file.

Figure 3.4
Field Grade Officers Appointed as Joint Qualified Officers, by Service and Fiscal Year—
Percentage

	2008	2009	2010	2011	2012	2013	2014	2015	2016	2017
Air Force	1.3	1.7	2.3	1.9	1.1	1.7	1.5	1.7	1.6	1.1
Army	1.3	1.2	2.1	1.4	1.2	1.5	1.2	1.3	1.4	1.4
Marine Corps	1.4	1.6	2.8	2.5	2.2	2.4	1.8	2.0	2.2	1.7
Navy	1.4	1.4	2.5	1.4	1.5	1.3	1.3	1.5	1.3	1.1

SOURCE: Longitudinal data files created from JDAMIS and the officer master file.

Trends by Occupations

The services differ in relative portions of their officer corps that serve in tactical operations occupations.[2] As is shown in Table 3.2, the Army has a considerably higher percentage of officers in nontactical operations specialties. We examined whether these service differences have an impact on JQO inventory and annual appointee findings.

Figures 3.5 through 3.8 show differences in inventory based on occupation. The overall trends observed are as follows:

- The Army's high percentage of nontactical operations officers is reflected in the number of JQOs in their respective overall inventory. This prevalence of nontactical operations JQOs is similar but not as stark for the Air Force. Despite the Navy having a percentage of nontactical operations occupations that is similar to that of the Air Force, the Navy stands out from all other services in that its JQO inventory numbers are more dominated by tactical operations JQOs (Figure 3.5).
- When normalizing all numbers by the size of the respective officer corps, the percentages tell a different story, as is shown in Figure 3.6. On a percentage basis, all services have higher portions of their tactical operations officers qualified as JQOs.[3] Over the ten-year period that we examined, the consistently increasing

Table 3.2
Service Differences for Officers Serving in Tactical Operations Occupations

Occupational Distinction	Air Force	Army	Marine Corps	Navy	Total
Tactical operations	40%	23%	58%	41%	36%
Nontactical operations	60%	77%	42%	59%	64%

SOURCE: Longitudinal data files created from JDAMIS and the officer master file.

---

[2] DoDI 1312.1-1, *Occupational Conversion Index: Enlisted/Officer/Civilian*, March 2001. This instruction was the basis for categorizing occupations into tactical operations and nontactical operations groupings. The DoD index reflects an occupation coding structure, designed to group similar occupations from one or more populations into a logical and consistent structure suitable for a variety of analytical purposes. Each military service has placed its occupations within this DoD taxonomy. Tactical operations occupations are all military specialties given the DoD occupational area code prefix 22, used to designate "Tactical Operations Officers" such as pilots, operations staff, and ground and naval arms officers. Nontactical operations occupations include all others, which are composed of the following occupational areas: "Intelligence Officers," "Engineering and Maintenance Officers," "Scientists and Professionals," "Health Care Officers," "Administrators," and "Supply, Procurement, and Allied Officers."

[3] Our categorization of nontactical operations officers includes professional officers, a category that comprises medical officers, judge advocates, and chaplains, for example. To the extent that the services have different percentages of their nontactical operations officers in professional fields (e.g., the Marine Corps does not have medical officers), these comparisons may be affected. However, acknowledging this caveat, and for purposes of completeness, we did not limit nontactical operations officers by excluding officers in the professional fields.

Figure 3.5
Field Grade Officer Joint Qualified Officer Inventory, by Service, Occupational Code, and Fiscal Year—Number

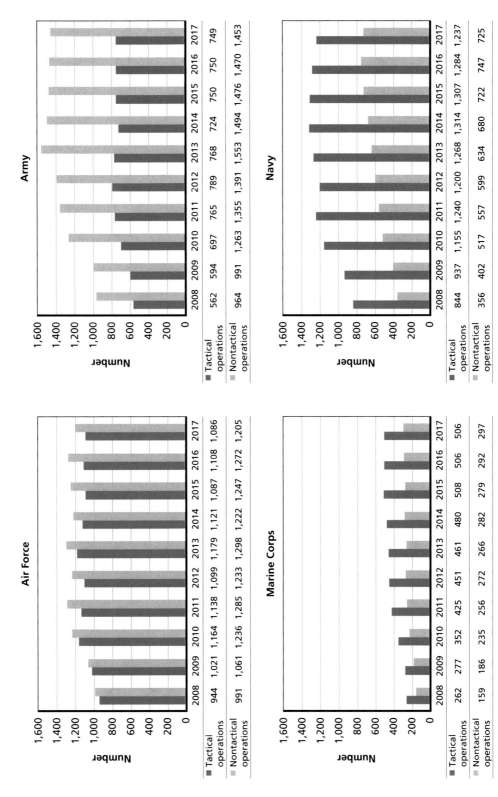

SOURCE: Longitudinal data files created from JDAMIS and the officer master file.

Figure 3.6
Field Grade Officer Joint Qualified Officer Inventory, by Service, Occupational Code, and Fiscal Year—Percentage

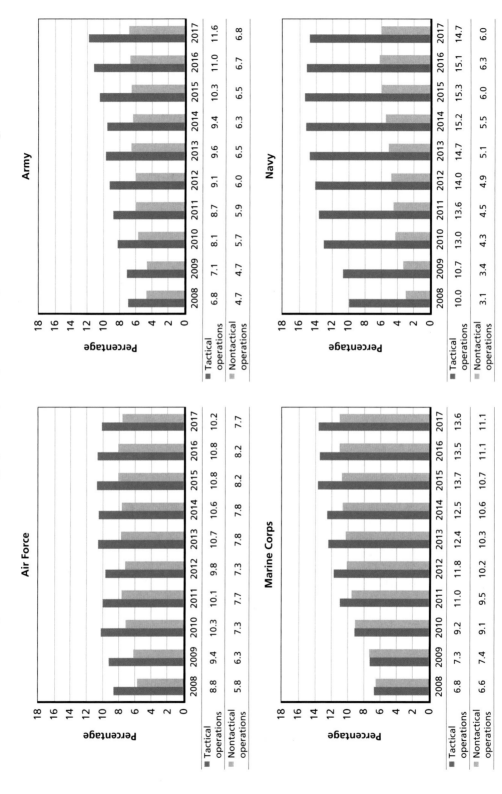

Air Force

	2008	2009	2010	2011	2012	2013	2014	2015	2016	2017
Tactical operations	8.8	9.4	10.3	10.1	9.8	10.7	10.6	10.8	10.8	10.2
Nontactical operations	5.8	6.3	7.3	7.7	7.3	7.8	7.8	8.2	8.2	7.7

Army

	2008	2009	2010	2011	2012	2013	2014	2015	2016	2017
Tactical operations	6.8	7.1	8.1	8.7	9.1	9.6	9.4	10.3	11.0	11.6
Nontactical operations	4.7	4.7	5.7	5.9	6.0	6.5	6.3	6.5	6.7	6.8

Marine Corps

	2008	2009	2010	2011	2012	2013	2014	2015	2016	2017
Tactical operations	6.8	7.3	9.2	11.0	11.8	12.4	12.5	13.7	13.5	13.6
Nontactical operations	6.6	7.4	9.1	9.5	10.2	10.3	10.6	10.7	11.1	11.1

Navy

	2008	2009	2010	2011	2012	2013	2014	2015	2016	2017
Tactical operations	10.0	10.7	13.0	13.6	14.0	14.7	15.2	15.3	15.1	14.7
Nontactical operations	3.1	3.4	4.3	4.5	4.9	5.1	5.5	6.0	6.3	6.0

SOURCE: Longitudinal data files created from JDAMIS and the officer master file.

percentage of tactical operations officers who have become JQOs is striking—with the exception of the Air Force, which has a relatively flat percentage over time. Looking exclusively at tactical operations officers in FY 2017, the Navy has a higher percentage of such officers designated as JQOs—about 15 percent, compared with about 11 percent for the Air Force and Army.

- For nontactical operations officer JQO inventories in 2017, the Marine Corps has the highest qualified rates, at over 11 percent, with all other services ranging from 6 percent to 8 percent.
- During the 2010 grandfathering period associated with implementing the recency requirement for E-JDA joint experience, Army nontactical operations officers and Navy tactical operations officers were particularly adept at getting appointed as JQOs (Figures 3.7 and 3.8).
- There does not appear to be an evident trend associated with occupational distinction and the number or percentage of annual JQO appointees that is different from the previously mentioned overall decline in numbers.

Trends by Grade

Figures 3.9 and 3.10 depict inventories by grade (O-4, O-5, and O-6). The trends and observations noted for the overall inventory are similarly observed for annual appointees, so we show data only for overall inventory. The overall trends observed for JQO inventory by grade are as follows:

- The number of O-6 JQOs has exceeded the numbers for all other grades in nearly all years. This is especially true in the Army and Navy, mostly true for the Marine Corps, and to a much lesser degree for the Air Force. In recent years the Army has had the largest inventory of JQO O-6s, at almost 1,400 in FY 2017—over 200 more than the Air Force or Navy in the same year. Changes in O-6 JQO inventory over recent times show that the Marine Corps and Navy have consistently shown the greater gains.
- The Air Force has consistently had greater numbers of both O-5 and O-4 JQO inventories than the other services. In fact, for the FY 2008 to FY 2010 time frame, the Air Force had even more O-5 than O-6 JQOs. The Army and Navy have a similar pattern and number of O-5 JQOs when compared with each other, but their totals are considerably lower (by about 200) than those of Air Force O-5 JQOs.
- Within the respective service grade categories, the percentage of O-6 JQOs has grown substantially and consistently over the ten-year period. For the Air Force, Army, and Navy, these increases have gone from 15–20 percent of their O-6 officer corps in FY 2008 to 30–35 percent in FY 2017. The Marine Corps has made

Figure 3.7
Field Grade Officers Appointed as Joint Qualified Officers, by Service, Occupational Code, and Fiscal Year—Number

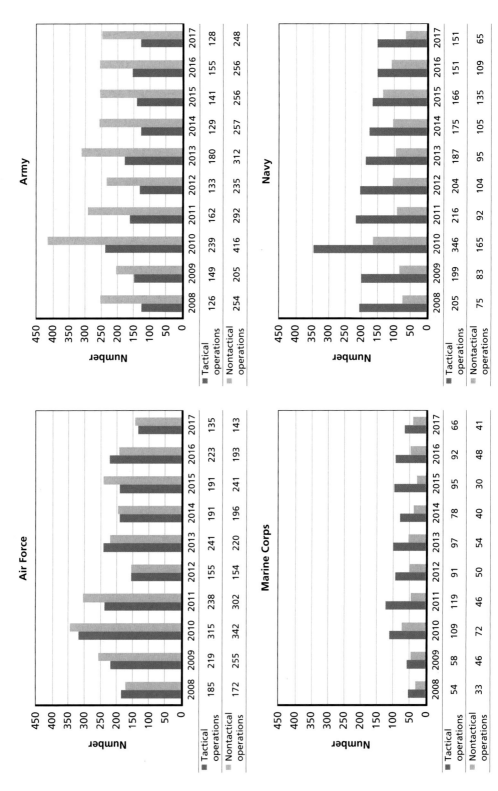

Air Force

	2008	2009	2010	2011	2012	2013	2014	2015	2016	2017
Tactical operations	185	219	315	238	155	241	191	191	223	135
Nontactical operations	172	255	342	302	154	220	196	241	193	143

Army

	2008	2009	2010	2011	2012	2013	2014	2015	2016	2017
Tactical operations	126	149	239	162	133	180	129	141	155	128
Nontactical operations	254	205	416	292	235	312	257	256	256	248

Marine Corps

	2008	2009	2010	2011	2012	2013	2014	2015	2016	2017
Tactical operations	54	58	109	119	91	97	78	95	92	66
Nontactical operations	33	46	72	46	50	54	40	30	48	41

Navy

	2008	2009	2010	2011	2012	2013	2014	2015	2016	2017
Tactical operations	205	199	346	216	204	187	175	166	151	151
Nontactical operations	75	83	165	92	104	95	105	135	109	65

SOURCE: Longitudinal data files created from JDAMIS and the officer master file.

Figure 3.8
Field Grade Officers Appointed as Joint Qualified Officers, by Service, Occupational Code, and Fiscal Year—Percentage

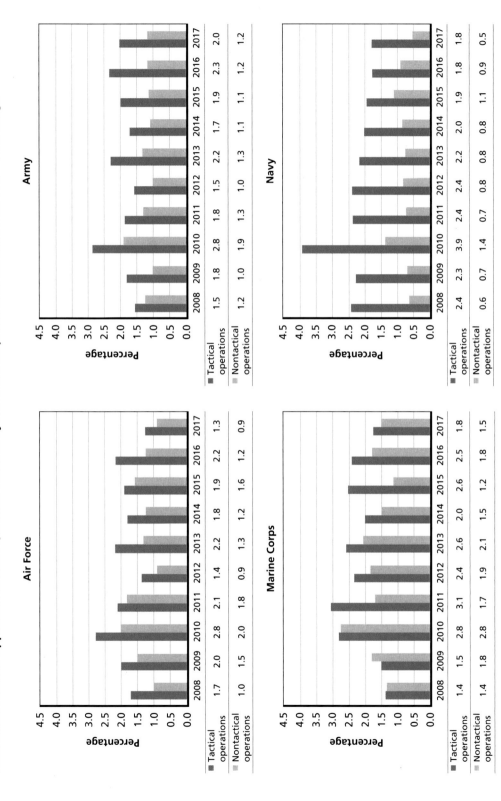

SOURCE: Longitudinal data files created from JDAMIS and the officer master file.

Figure 3.9
Field Grade Officer Joint Qualified Officer Inventory, by Service, Grade, and Fiscal Year—Number

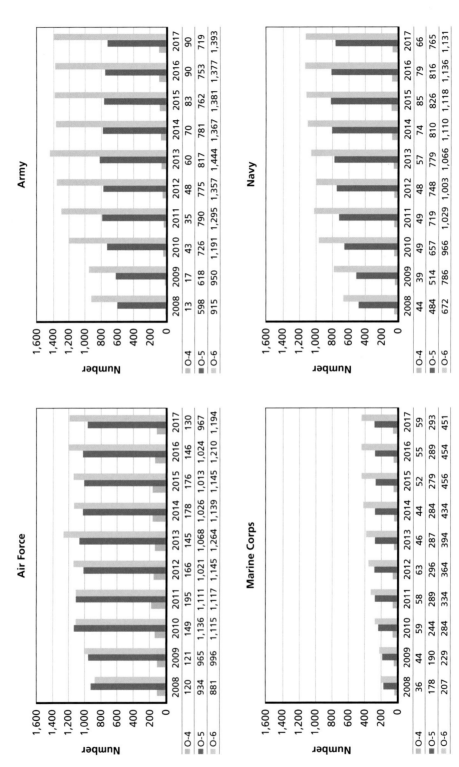

Army

	2008	2009	2010	2011	2012	2013	2014	2015	2016	2017
O-4	13	17	43	35	48	60	70	83	90	90
O-5	598	618	726	790	775	817	781	762	753	719
O-6	915	950	1,191	1,295	1,357	1,444	1,367	1,381	1,377	1,393

Navy

	2008	2009	2010	2011	2012	2013	2014	2015	2016	2017
O-4	44	39	49	49	48	57	74	85	79	66
O-5	484	514	657	719	748	779	810	826	816	765
O-6	672	786	966	1,029	1,003	1,066	1,110	1,118	1,136	1,131

Air Force

	2008	2009	2010	2011	2012	2013	2014	2015	2016	2017
O-4	120	121	149	195	166	145	178	176	146	130
O-5	934	965	1,136	1,111	1,021	1,068	1,026	1,013	1,024	967
O-6	881	996	1,115	1,117	1,145	1,264	1,139	1,145	1,210	1,194

Marine Corps

	2008	2009	2010	2011	2012	2013	2014	2015	2016	2017
O-4	36	44	59	58	63	46	44	52	55	59
O-5	178	190	244	289	296	287	284	279	289	293
O-6	207	229	284	334	364	394	434	456	454	451

SOURCE: Longitudinal data files created from JDAMIS and the officer master file.

Figure 3.10
Field Grade Officer Joint Qualified Officer Inventory, by Service, Grade, and Fiscal Year—Percentage

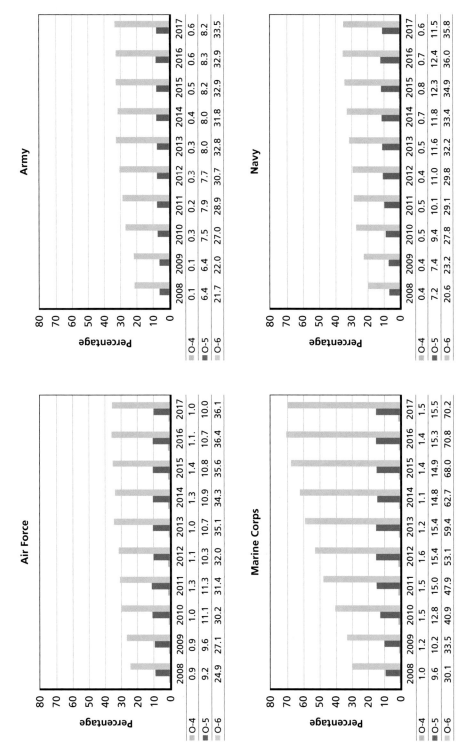

SOURCE: Longitudinal data files created from JDAMIS and the officer master file.

Air Force

	2008	2009	2010	2011	2012	2013	2014	2015	2016	2017
O-4	0.9	0.9	1.0	1.3	1.1	1.0	1.3	1.4	1.1.	1.0
O-5	9.2	9.6	11.1	11.3	10.3	10.7	10.9	10.8	10.7	10.0
O-6	24.9	27.1	30.2	31.4	32.0	35.1	34.3	35.6	36.4	36.1

Army

	2008	2009	2010	2011	2012	2013	2014	2015	2016	2017
O-4	0.1	0.1	0.3	0.2	0.3	0.3	0.4	0.5	0.6	0.6
O-5	6.4	6.4	7.5	7.9	7.7	8.0	8.0	8.2	8.3	8.2
O-6	21.7	22.0	27.0	28.9	30.7	32.8	31.8	32.9	32.9	33.5

Marine Corps

	2008	2009	2010	2011	2012	2013	2014	2015	2016	2017
O-4	1.0	1.2	1.5	1.5	1.6	1.2	1.1	1.4	1.4	1.5
O-5	9.6	10.2	12.8	15.0	15.4	15.4	14.8	14.9	15.3	15.5
O-6	30.1	33.5	40.9	47.9	53.1	59.4	62.7	68.0	70.8	70.2

Navy

	2008	2009	2010	2011	2012	2013	2014	2015	2016	2017
O-4	0.4	0.4	0.5	0.5	0.4	0.5	0.7	0.8	0.7	0.6
O-5	7.2	7.4	9.4	10.1	11.0	11.6	11.8	12.3	12.4	11.5
O-6	20.6	23.2	27.8	29.1	29.8	32.2	33.4	34.9	36.0	35.8

even greater gains over this time period: in FY 2017 over 70 percent of Marine Corps O-6s were designated as JQOs.

- Relatively stable percentage trends were noted for both the O-4 and O-5 JQO inventories over the ten-year time frame.
- Further breakdowns by the categories of tactical operations versus nontactical operations did not note any additional observations that were unique or different from prior observations.

CHAPTER FOUR

Education and Experience Requirements

Becoming a Level III JQO is a function of successfully completing both JPME requirements and job experience (achieved through either an S-JDA or accumulation of a sufficient number of points resulting from a more limited joint assignment supplemented with discretionary points—i.e., an E-JDA). In this chapter we examine the trends associated with both of these education and experience components.

Accomplishing JPME-II

As is shown in Table 2.2, multiple institutions focus on senior officer PME (primarily O-5s and O-6s). With the NDAA for FY 2007, Congress authorized senior service PME institutions to confer JPME-II status on their graduates similar to the senior joint PME institutions. The CJCSI

> recognizes both the distinctiveness and interdependence of joint and service schools in officer education. Service schools, in keeping with their role of developing service specialists, place emphasis on education primarily from a service perspective in accordance with joint learning areas and objectives. Joint schools emphasize joint education from a joint perspective.[1]

Given that all institutions have the same focus, learning areas, objectives, and expected outcomes, for analytical purposes we combined all SSSs into a single category, pooled all SJSs with the same instructional duration into a single category (to include the follow-on Joint Advanced Warfighting School), and retained the JCWS separately because it is only a ten-week program of instruction.[2]

---

[1] CJCSI 1800.01E, 2015a.

[2] Senior service schools include the Air War College, Army War College, Marine Corps War College, and College of Naval Warfare. Senior joint schools include National War College, Dwight D. Eisenhower School for National Security and Resource Strategy (formerly the Industrial College of the Armed Forces), College of International Security Affairs, and Joint Advanced Warfighting School.

Table 4.1
Graduates from JPME-II Granting Institutions

| | Number and Percentage of Graduates | | | | | | |
| | JCWS | | SJSs | | SSSs | | Total |
Fiscal Year	N	%	N	%	N	%	N
2008	880	54%	288	18%	453	28%	1,621
2009	873	54%	277	17%	462	29%	1,612
2010	861	54%	280	18%	453	28%	1,594
2011	868	55%	286	18%	424	27%	1,578
2012	880	56%	294	19%	403	26%	1,577
2013	879	56%	286	18%	399	26%	1,564
2014	881	56%	286	18%	407	26%	1,574
2015	911	56%	286	18%	433	27%	1,630
2016	792	53%	304	20%	402	27%	1,498
2017	750	56%	252	19%	336	25%	1,338

SOURCE: Longitudinal data files created from JDAMIS and the officer master file.
NOTE: The annual number of JPME-II graduates in this table reflect graduates in these time periods only and are not related to future JQO status. These numbers are taken from JDAMIS on a fiscal year basis; therefore, they may differ from what institutions typically report on an academic year (August–July) basis. However, trends over time should be consistent.

Table 4.1 reports the number and percentage of graduates by fiscal year for these three categories of JPME-II granting institutions. During this ten-year time period, around 1,600 JPME-II degrees were conferred each year; the fewest number of graduates was in FY 2017, with just over 1,300. It is not yet evident whether this is the beginning of a downward trend. On a yearly basis, the JCWS produces about 55 percent or more of all JPME-II graduates. Similarly, the SJSs and SSSs produce constant percentages, about 17–20 percent and 25–29 percent, respectively.

Differences in graduate production are the result of several conditions. First, the JCWS is the educator of choice for those services or officers that desire a shorter program of instruction—ten weeks versus ten months. Second, the JCWS is considerably less costly (both in time and dollars) for the parent service. Third, depending on the requirements of the service and individual officer, the JCWS is the only JPME-II option for younger field grade officers (specifically O-4s). Fourth, the services use highly competitive selection methods to assign officers to SJSs and SSSs, leaving the JCWS as the JPME-II pathway for the remainder of O-5s and O-6s who are not selected for senior educational programs. Finally, given the shorter course duration, the JCWS is able to offer considerably more convenings on an annual basis and thereby able to yield greater numbers of graduates for manageable class sizes.

Despite changes in JPME policy and options over the last ten years, the consistency in percentages of graduates produced from the respective senior institutions is striking. While the absolute number of graduates varies over time, the relative percentage of graduates across institutions has only limited variance. If leadership were to consider noteworthy changes to these past consistent student assignment levels, it is questionable whether the service and SJSs could scale their offerings and infrastructure in a timely manner to cover significant adjustments while retaining sufficient quality of instruction and class sizes.

In framing a strategic approach for joint officer management, Harry J. Thie and colleagues made an observation that JPME-II seats were limited and thereby may be constraining the number of officers being designated as joint specialty officers.[3] While resources may be an issue, the decline in the number of annual JPME-II graduates across the conferring educational institutions shows that there certainly is some capacity to either surge or expand.

Joint Professional Military Education (Phase II) Granting Institutions for Joint Qualified Officers

We now turn to the historical distribution of institutional JPME-II graduates within the annual inventory of JQOs. Figures 4.1 and 4.2 show the JPME-II granting institution for the annual inventory of JQOs. These figures illustrate the inventory trends for both the absolute number of graduates and the overall percentage of graduates by institution on an annual basis.

The JCWS has consistently been the primary source of JPME-II graduates in the annual JQO inventory. As is shown in Figure 4.1, the number of JCWS graduates exceeds the number of JPME-II graduates from both SJSs and SSSs combined, by a factor of at least two. However, the percentage of JQOs completing JPME-II at the JCWS has been declining over the last ten years, as is shown in Figure 4.2. While SJSs have steadily had about 15 percent of JPME-II graduates, the number of JQOs graduating with JPME-II from SSSs has increased—reflecting the 2007 change allowing SSSs to confer JPME-II graduations. Accordingly, the services have used this policy primarily at that expense of sending students to the JCWS; moreover, since 2013 the number of SSS graduates in the JQO annual cohort has increasingly exceeded the number of SJS graduates.

Figures 4.3 and 4.4 illustrate the same concepts but show the number of officers appointed as JQOs in a given year versus the historical accumulated inventory (akin to annual production versus rolling averages). In these figures, the trends tend to have more annual variance but support the same outcomes and conclusions as Figures 4.1 and 4.2. These numbers serve as leading indicators, and therefore it appears that future trends involving increased SSS production of JPME-II graduates will only continue.

---

3   Thie, Harrell, Yardley, Oshiro, Potter, Schirmer, and Lim, 2005.

Figure 4.1
JPME-II Granting Institutions for Joint Qualified Officer Inventory, by Fiscal Year

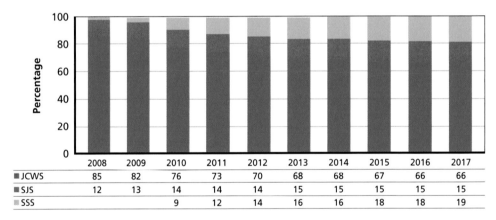

	2008	2009	2010	2011	2012	2013	2014	2015	2016	2017
JCWS	4,310	4,493	5,022	5,100	4,934	5,027	4,991	4,909	4,907	4,785
SJS	633	709	919	968	1,017	1,129	1,067	1,099	1,135	1,060
SSS	90	197	570	838	985	1,172	1,176	1,294	1,330	1,362

SOURCE: Longitudinal data files created from JDAMIS and the officer master file.
NOTE: Officers achieving JPME-II credit through other means are excluded from this analysis.

Figure 4.2
Percentage of Joint Qualified Officer Inventory, from JPME-II Granting Institutions, by Fiscal Year

	2008	2009	2010	2011	2012	2013	2014	2015	2016	2017
JCWS	85	82	76	73	70	68	68	67	66	66
SJS	12	13	14	14	14	15	15	15	15	15
SSS			9	12	14	16	16	18	18	19

SOURCE: Longitudinal data files created from JDAMIS and the officer master file.
NOTE: Percentages may not sum to 100% due to rounding and the fact that some officers achieve JPME-II credit through other means.

The military services use several educational venues for meeting JPME-II requirements, as illustrated in Figures 4.5 and 4.6. These graphs show both the absolute
number and percentage of the JQO inventory that graduated from respective JPME-II
institutions by fiscal year and service. Figure 4.6 shows a declining trend for percent-

Figure 4.3
JPME-II Granting Institution for Field Grade Officers Appointed as Joint Qualified Officers, by Fiscal Year

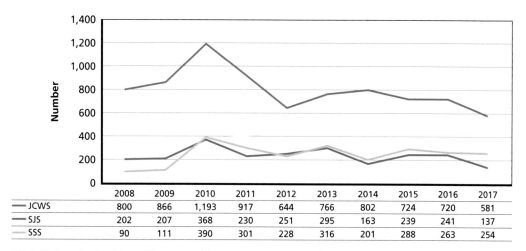

	2008	2009	2010	2011	2012	2013	2014	2015	2016	2017
JCWS	800	866	1,193	917	644	766	802	724	720	581
SJS	202	207	368	230	251	295	163	239	241	137
SSS	90	111	390	301	228	316	201	288	263	254

SOURCE: Longitudinal data files created from JDAMIS and the officer master file.
NOTE: Officers achieving JPME-II credit through other means are excluded from this analysis.

Figure 4.4
Percentage of Officers Appointed as Joint Qualified Officers from JPME-II Granting Institutions, by Fiscal Year

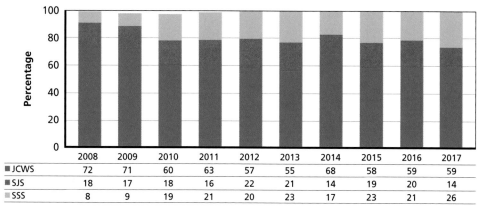

	2008	2009	2010	2011	2012	2013	2014	2015	2016	2017
JCWS	72	71	60	63	57	55	68	58	59	59
SJS	18	17	18	16	22	21	14	19	20	14
SSS	8	9	19	21	20	23	17	23	21	26

SOURCE: Longitudinal data files created from JDAMIS and the officer master file.
NOTE: Percentages may not sum to 100 due to rounding and because some officers achieve JPME-II credit through other means.

age of JCWS graduates composing the JQO inventory for all the services. Similarly, for each service, an increasing share of the JQO inventory is graduating from an SSS. This is especially true for the Army and Marine Corps, where in 2017 this percentage was 24 percent and 26 percent, respectively.

Figure 4.5
JPME-II Granting Institutions for Joint Qualified Officer Inventory, by Fiscal Year and Service—Number

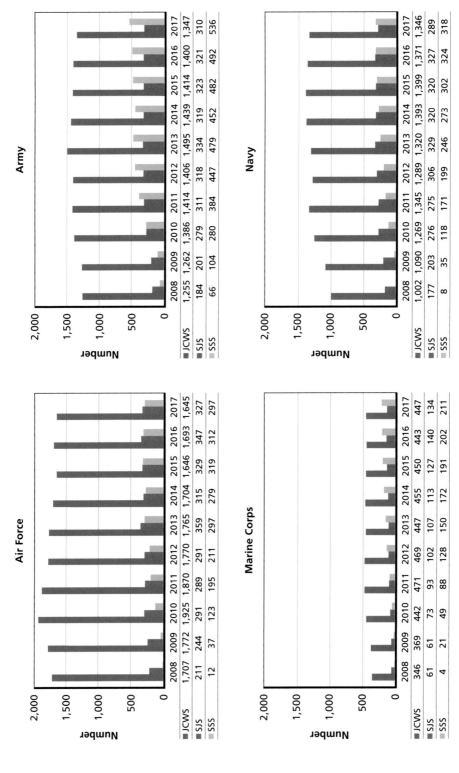

Air Force

	2008	2009	2010	2011	2012	2013	2014	2015	2016	2017
JCWS	1,707	1,772	1,925	1,870	1,770	1,765	1,704	1,646	1,693	1,645
SJS	211	244	291	289	291	359	315	329	347	327
SSS	12	37	123	195	211	297	279	319	312	297

Army

	2008	2009	2010	2011	2012	2013	2014	2015	2016	2017
JCWS	1,255	1,262	1,386	1,414	1,406	1,495	1,439	1,414	1,400	1,347
SJS	184	201	279	311	318	334	319	323	321	310
SSS	66	104	280	384	447	479	452	482	492	536

Marine Corps

	2008	2009	2010	2011	2012	2013	2014	2015	2016	2017
JCWS	346	369	442	471	469	447	455	450	443	447
SJS	61	61	73	93	102	107	113	127	140	134
SSS	4	21	49	88	128	150	172	191	202	211

Navy

	2008	2009	2010	2011	2012	2013	2014	2015	2016	2017
JCWS	1,002	1,090	1,269	1,345	1,289	1,320	1,393	1,399	1,371	1,346
SJS	177	203	276	275	306	329	320	320	327	289
SSS	8	35	118	171	199	246	273	302	324	318

SOURCE: Longitudinal data files created from JDAMIS and the officer master file.
NOTE: Officers achieving JPME-II credit through other means are excluded from this analysis.

Figure 4.6
JPME-II Granting Institutions for Joint Qualified Officer Inventory, by Fiscal Year and Service—Percentage

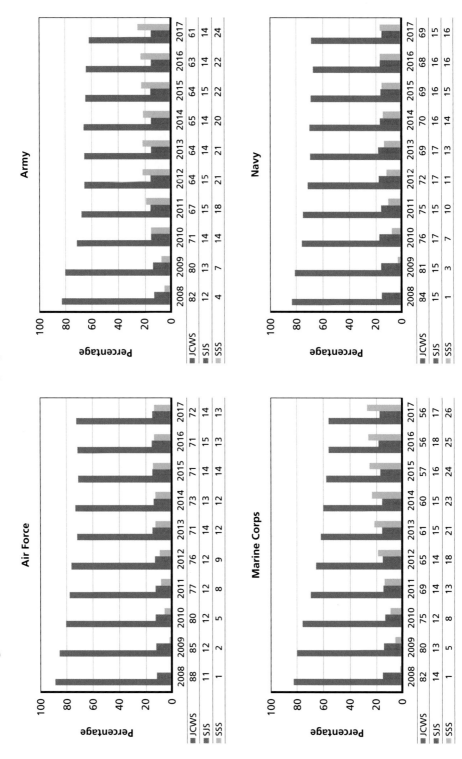

SOURCE: Longitudinal data files created from JDAMIS and the officer master file.
NOTE: Officers achieving JPME-II credit through other means are excluded from this analysis.

Figure 4.7
JPME-II Granting Institutions for Joint Qualified Officer Inventory, by Service and Grade,
Fiscal Year 2017

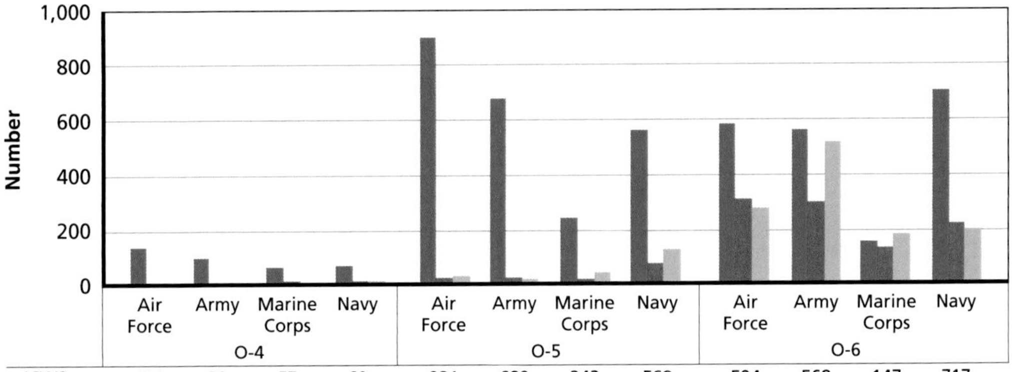

	Air Force	Army	Marine Corps	Navy	Air Force	Army	Marine Corps	Navy	Air Force	Army	Marine Corps	Navy
			O-4				O-5				O-6	
■ JCWS	130	90	57	60	921	689	243	569	594	568	147	717
■ SJS	0	0	1	2	16	14	10	70	311	296	123	217
■ SSS	0	0	0	1	24	13	36	122	273	523	175	195

SOURCE: Longitudinal data files created from JDAMIS and the officer master file.
NOTE: Officers achieving JPME-II credit through other means are excluded from this analysis.

In the O-4 and O-5 grades, the services predominantly use the combination of the JCWS and joint experience to develop JQOs, as Figure 4.7 illustrates. Differences in service approaches are readily visible. The Air Force produces more O-4 JQOs than do the other services, indicating a higher priority for combining JPME-II and joint experience at more junior levels.

Figure 4.8 shows the JPME-II institution for officers appointed as JQOs in FY 2017 by grade. As expected, the JCWS educates all O-4 JQOs and the vast majority of O-5 JQOs. Service preferences become quite evident at the grade of O-6, however. Most striking, the Army used the SSS to create O-6 JQOs at a much greater number than the other services. This suggests that the Army focused on the accomplishment of joint experience first and subsequently accomplished the JPME-II requirement through an SSS later in a career. At the other extreme, the Navy still used the JCWS extensively to create O-6 JQOs while placing less emphasis on SJSs and SSSs as the source of JPME-II instruction.

Achieving Joint Experience

The traditional path for achieving joint experience for most officers is via a full joint duty credit assignment (i.e., completion of an uninterrupted 36-month JDAL assignment). As was described in Chapter Three, the NDAA for FY 2007 paved the way for the E-JDA point-based system. This section examines the trends in accomplishing the joint experience requirement for those who are designated as JQOs—comparing the

Figure 4.8
JPME-II Granting Institutions Appointed as Joint Qualified Officers, by Service and Grade,
Fiscal Year 2017

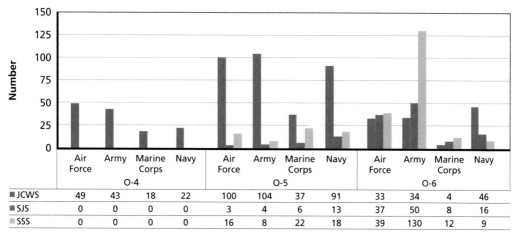

	Air Force	Army	Marine Corps	Navy	Air Force	Army	Marine Corps	Navy	Air Force	Army	Marine Corps	Navy
		O-4				O-5				O-6		
JCWS	49	43	18	22	100	104	37	91	33	34	4	46
SJS	0	0	0	0	3	4	6	13	37	50	8	16
SSS	0	0	0	0	16	8	22	18	39	130	12	9

SOURCE: Longitudinal data files created from JDAMIS and the officer master file.
NOTE: Officers achieving JPME-II credit through other means are excluded from this analysis.

S-JDA and E-JDA assignment paths. The issues of waivers to a full joint duty credit assignment will be addressed in Chapter Five.

Figure 4.9 shows that, after an initial lag associated with implementing a justifiable joint qualification points process in FY 2007, the percentage of individuals using E-JDA climbed quickly in the first few years. The percentages stabilized for three

Figure 4.9
Joint Duty Assignment Path for Individuals Appointed as Joint Qualified Officers,
by Fiscal Year

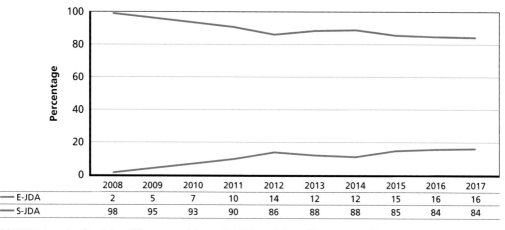

	2008	2009	2010	2011	2012	2013	2014	2015	2016	2017
E-JDA	2	5	7	10	14	12	12	15	16	16
S-JDA	98	95	93	90	86	88	88	85	84	84

SOURCE: Longitudinal data files created from JDAMIS and the officer master file.

years, increased in FY 2015 to around 16 percent, and have since been relatively steady. The future distribution between S-JDA and E-JDA assignment paths will depend on the number of future joint operations that require extended individual deployments in which the person earns HFP or IDP and the diligence with which officers complete E-JDA applications.

Decomposing these overall observations by service in Figure 4.10 demonstrates that the Army has made the greatest use of the E-JDA option. During the ten-year period examined, the Army's percentage of individuals using E-JDA increased progressively from 3 percent in FY 2008 to 29 percent in FY 2017. The other services have

Figure 4.10
Joint Duty Assignment Path for Individuals Appointed as Joint Qualified Officers, by Fiscal Year and Service

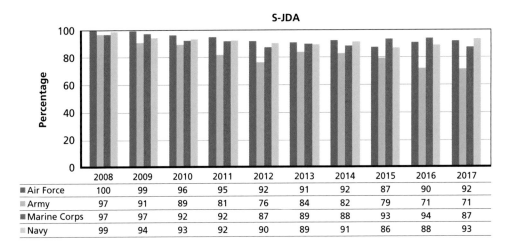

S-JDA

	2008	2009	2010	2011	2012	2013	2014	2015	2016	2017
Air Force	100	99	96	95	92	91	92	87	90	92
Army	97	91	89	81	76	84	82	79	71	71
Marine Corps	97	97	92	92	87	89	88	93	94	87
Navy	99	94	93	92	90	89	91	86	88	93

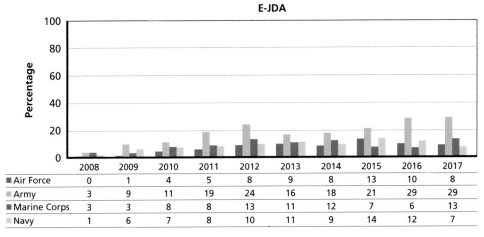

E-JDA

	2008	2009	2010	2011	2012	2013	2014	2015	2016	2017
Air Force	0	1	4	5	8	9	8	13	10	8
Army	3	9	11	19	24	16	18	21	29	29
Marine Corps	3	3	8	8	13	11	12	7	6	13
Navy	1	6	7	8	10	11	9	14	12	7

SOURCE: Longitudinal data files created from JDAMIS and the officer master file.

essentially been in lockstep; there are only a few percentage points difference between them, but the increase was much slower and stabilized at around 15 percent in FY 2017. Notably, the Army's increased use of E-JDA occurred during a time in which combat deployments declined significantly. Appreciating that there is a lag in achieving JQO status after an assignment, there is still an open question as to whether services with significantly more combat-related deployments are able to have more (or fewer) of their officers successfully accomplish the joint experience requirement associated with an E-JDA path.

Figure 4.11 looks further at the E-JDA path for achieving JQO designation, presenting the percentage of officers by service and grade who used the E-JDA path to gain JQO (the complementary percentage of officers using the S-JDA route would be the balance of 100 percent). It is evident that while in the aggregate the Army makes the greatest use of the E-JDA path to gaining JQO status, this path is predominantly employed by Army O-6s, with 45 percent and 41 percent of all Army O-6s being appointed as JQOs in FY 2016 and FY 2017, respectively, via this path.

No grade in any other service was found to come even close to these consistently high results for the Army, except for what appears to be an aberrant one-year result of 27 percent for Navy O-4s in FY 2015. We also examined these trends for tactical operations versus nontactical operations occupations. The results were the same except for nontactical operations occupations showing a lag of almost two years in achieving greater use of the E-JDA path compared with tactical operations occupations.

The final category we examined for joint experience paths was the JPME-II granting institution. We compared the percentage of JQOs who used S-JDA or E-JDA experience paths for each of the three JPME-II institution types. These findings are noted in Figures 4.12 and 4.13 for both the full JQO inventory and annual appointees, respectively.

It is evident across all JPME-II institution types that E-JDA percentages are increasing (and all S-JDA percentages are correspondingly decreasing). The greatest increase in E-JDA utilization are for the SSSs (increasing from 1 percent in FY 2008 to 21 percent in FY 2017), followed by the SJSs (increasing from 3 percent in FY 2008 to 17 percent in FY 2017). The JCWS had the least movement during this ten-year period, having stabilized at about 6 percent to 8 percent E-JDA utilization for JQO inventory over the last three years. These trends are essentially the same whether for the overall JQO inventory or annual appointees.

The services fill JDAL positions at roughly the same rate as that shown in Table 4.2, except for the Navy, which fills at a higher rate of about 67 percent of its assigned joint billets. If the services also ensured that officers in JDAL positions completed JPME-II at the same points in their careers, we would expect to see more JQOs emerge from some services (particularly the Army and Navy) than we see in the data.

Figure 4.11
E-JDA Path Percentages for Being Appointed as a Joint Qualified Officer, by Fiscal Year, Service, and Grade

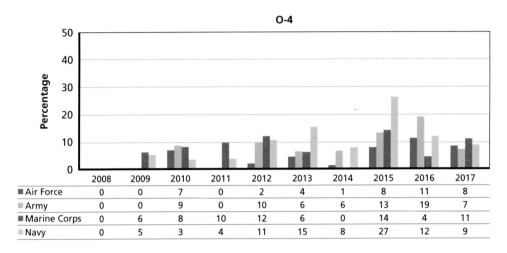

O-4

	2008	2009	2010	2011	2012	2013	2014	2015	2016	2017
■ Air Force	0	0	7	0	2	4	1	8	11	8
■ Army	0	0	9	0	10	6	6	13	19	7
■ Marine Corps	0	6	8	10	12	6	0	14	4	11
■ Navy	0	5	3	4	11	15	8	27	12	9

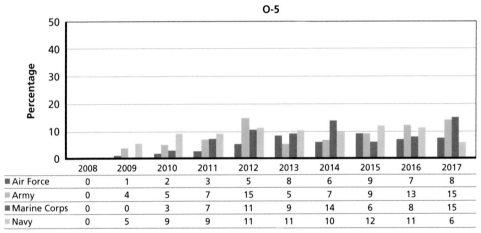

O-5

	2008	2009	2010	2011	2012	2013	2014	2015	2016	2017
■ Air Force	0	1	2	3	5	8	6	9	7	8
■ Army	0	4	5	7	15	5	7	9	13	15
■ Marine Corps	0	0	3	7	11	9	14	6	8	15
■ Navy	0	5	9	9	11	11	10	12	11	6

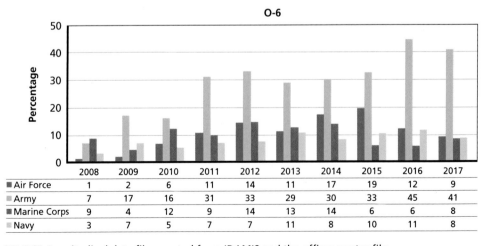

O-6

	2008	2009	2010	2011	2012	2013	2014	2015	2016	2017
■ Air Force	1	2	6	11	14	11	17	19	12	9
■ Army	7	17	16	31	33	29	30	33	45	41
■ Marine Corps	9	4	12	9	14	13	14	6	6	8
■ Navy	3	7	5	7	7	11	8	10	11	8

SOURCE: Longitudinal data files created from JDAMIS and the officer master file.

Figure 4.12
**S-JDA Versus E-JDA Paths for Joint Qualified Officer Inventory and JPME-II Granting
Institution, by Fiscal Year**

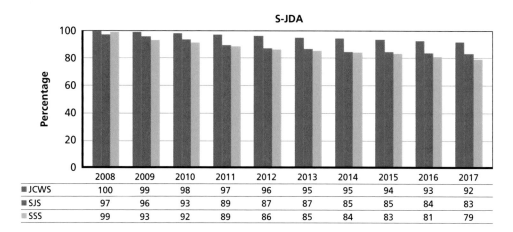

S-JDA

	2008	2009	2010	2011	2012	2013	2014	2015	2016	2017
■ JCWS	100	99	98	97	96	95	95	94	93	92
■ SJS	97	96	93	89	87	87	85	85	84	83
■ SSS	99	93	92	89	86	85	84	83	81	79

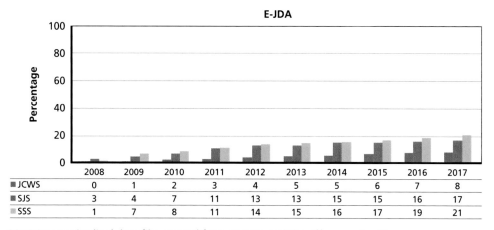

E-JDA

	2008	2009	2010	2011	2012	2013	2014	2015	2016	2017
■ JCWS	0	1	2	3	4	5	5	6	7	8
■ SJS	3	4	7	11	13	13	15	15	16	17
■ SSS	1	7	8	11	14	15	16	17	19	21

SOURCE: Longitudinal data files created from JDAMIS and the officer master file.

Table 4.2
FY 2017 Assigned and Filled Joint Billets for Field Grade Officers

	Air Force	Army	Marine Corps	Navy	Total
Joint billets filled	2,026	2,088	413	1,587	6,114
Joint billets assigned	3,622	3,551	768	2,382	10,323
Joint fill rate	56%	59%	54%	67%	59%
Service share of joint billets	35%	34%	8%	23%	100%
Service share of billets filled	33%	34%	7%	26%	100%

SOURCE: Joint Staff J1, April 3, 2017.

Figure 4.13
S-JDA Versus E-JDA Paths for Officers Appointed as Joint Qualified Officers, and JPME-II Granting Institution, by Fiscal Year

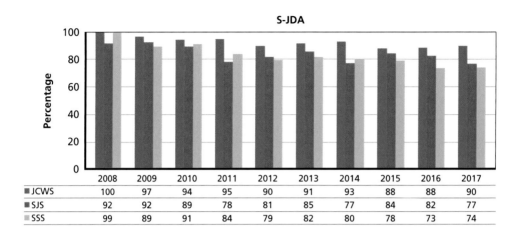

S-JDA	2008	2009	2010	2011	2012	2013	2014	2015	2016	2017
JCWS	100	97	94	95	90	91	93	88	88	90
SJS	92	92	89	78	81	85	77	84	82	77
SSS	99	89	91	84	79	82	80	78	73	74

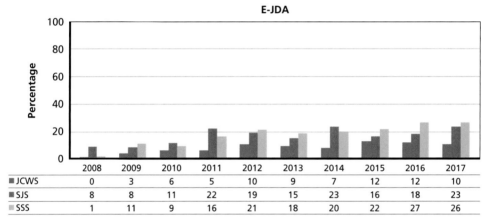

E-JDA	2008	2009	2010	2011	2012	2013	2014	2015	2016	2017
JCWS	0	3	6	5	10	9	7	12	12	10
SJS	8	8	11	22	19	15	23	16	18	23
SSS	1	11	9	16	21	18	20	22	27	26

SOURCE: Longitudinal data files created from JDAMIS and the officer master file.

Recall that the joint experience component of E-JDA is calculated as a function of an assignment's combat intensity and duration. The combat intensity multiplier is binary and determined based on an officer receiving HFP or IDP.[4] The military services report previous year expenditures and future year requirements for HFP and IDP

---

[4]   CJCSI 1330.05A provides specific guidance in that the combat intensity multiplier "is correlated to the receipt of hostile fire/imminent danger pay." HFD and IDP are payable at the monthly rate of $225. Service members will receive $7.50 for each day they are on duty in an IDP area up to the maximum monthly rate of $225. Members who are exposed to a hostile fire or hostile mine explosion event are eligible to receive nonprorated HFP in the full monthly amount of $225. Members cannot receive both HFP and IDP in the same month. CJCSI 1330.05A, 2015b, p. G-4.

Figure 4.14
Annual Hostile Fire Pay Expenditure, by Service

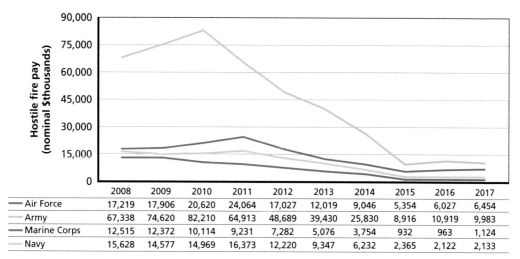

	2008	2009	2010	2011	2012	2013	2014	2015	2016	2017
—— Air Force	17,219	17,906	20,620	24,064	17,027	12,019	9,046	5,354	6,027	6,454
—— Army	67,338	74,620	82,210	64,913	48,689	39,430	25,830	8,916	10,919	9,983
—— Marine Corps	12,515	12,372	10,114	9,231	7,282	5,076	3,754	932	963	1,124
—— Navy	15,628	14,577	14,969	16,373	12,220	9,347	6,232	2,365	2,122	2,133

SOURCE: Current and archived budget submissions for each branch of the services: Deputy Assistant
Secretary of the Army—Budget, undated; U.S. Air Force, Financial Management and Comptroller,
undated; and U.S. Department of the Navy, undated.

in their annual military personnel budget submissions.[5] Data from official sources
show that the Army HFP peaked in FY 2010 at over $82 million and declined sharply
to a low of slightly less than $10 million in FY 2017, as is shown in Figure 4.14. All
other services showed declines in HFP, but they were nowhere near as steep. Contrary
to expectation, at a time when combat deployments declined overall, an increasing percentage of Army officers who deployed met the E-JDA criteria.

Figure 4.15 shows normalized HFP per officer for each military service.[6] Strik-
ingly, while all services since at least 2008 are at or around $225 per month in HFP,
implying relative constancy in combat deployments, the Army shows very large gains
in successful E-JDA applications (see Figure 4.10). More than other services, the Army
uses the E-JDA route to successfully create JQOs, even when deployment opportuni-
ties have declined steeply.

We appreciate that there is a lag between assignment completion and the formal
E-JDA package submission and approval. This lag may occur for a variety of reasons.

---

[5] For the current and archived budget submissions, which include these officer pays, see Deputy Assistant
Secretary of the Army—Budget, "Budget Materials," webpage, undated; U.S. Air Force, Financial Management
and Comptroller, "Air Force President's Budget FY20," webpage, undated; and U.S. Department of the Navy,
"Budget Materials," webpage, undated.

[6] The military services report average officer strength, or the average number of officers in the military service
on active duty during a given fiscal year. To determine HFP per officer, we divided the total HFP expenditures
for officers by the average officer strength.

Figure 4.15
Annual Hostile Fire Pay Per Officer, by Service

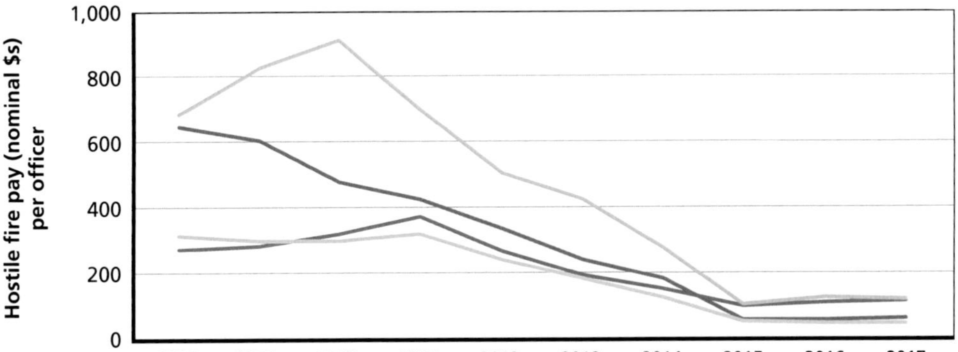

	2008	2009	2010	2011	2012	2013	2014	2015	2016	2017
—— Air Force	265	276	313	366	264	186	141	88	99	106
—— Army	685	827	913	697	504	419	273	97	117	109
—— Marine Corps	643	603	476	423	330	233	177	45	46	54
—— Navy	307	293	294	315	233	178	117	44	39	39

SOURCE: Longitudinal data files created from JDAMIS and the officer master file.

Before the E-JDA submission is complete, the service member must gather a host of supporting documents (performance evaluations, travel records, deployment awards, travel orders) that substantiate aspects of the E-JDA application. Some of those documents may not be available immediately following the deployment. Furthermore, the service member can submit the application up to a year after the end of the joint experience. A considerable amount of time is also needed for staff processing, where several levels of review between the service personnel centers and the Joint Staff validate the E-JDA submission. Decisions are published on a quarterly basis. In some situations, a successful E-JDA application may reflect an HFP-eligible deployment from up to two years earlier. As a result, an increase in HFP and IDP in 2010 (Figure 4.14) may explain an increase in successful E-JDA applications in 2012 (Figure 4.10).

For individuals using the E-JDA mode, the structure of joint deployments suggests two primary pathways through which officers may receive eventual credit: a unit-based JTF deployment and a joint individual augmentation (JIA) deployment. Joint doctrine establishes that a JTF should be composed first from an existing unit that has been tasked to form the foundation of the JTF. The JTF will emerge from a single-service organization, and the J1 staff will identify additional manpower requirements.[7] Officers with prominent command and staff responsibilities would be well-positioned for an eventual E-JDA, assuming their duties meet the requirements of joint matters.

---

[7] Joint Chiefs of Staff, *Joint Personnel Support*, Washington, D.C.: Joint Chiefs of Staff, Joint Publication 1-0, 2016, p. III-1.

The JTF J1 plans personnel support through a joint manning document, which provides a venue through which the combatant commander (CCDR) overseeing the JTF can validate personnel requirements and shortfalls. The CCDR fills any vacancies with assigned forces or other available means, with JIA support as the last possible option.[8] A CCDR submits any requirements for JIA support to the Joint Staff, where a multistep process determines the service that will satisfy the requirement.[9] Upon validation, approval, and sourcing, a service member deploys to the JTF in a JIA role. Depending on the scope of responsibilities, an officer filling a JIA deployment may qualify for an eventual E-JDA.

---

[8]   CJCSI 1301.01F, *Joint Individual Augmentation Procedures*, 2014, p. 2.

[9]   CJCSI 1301.01F, 2014, p. B-1.

CHAPTER FIVE

Sequencing of Joint Education and Joint Experience

Based on service and individual officer needs, the services employ various approaches for sequencing JPME-II with an S-JDA tour. In general, the service can enroll an officer in JPME-II before an S-JDA tour, in the midst of an S-JDA tour, or after an S-JDA tour. Depending on the particular sequence used, there can be differences in terms of which organization is responsible for funding and/or realizes the personnel loss due to education. We analyzed differences by JPME-II institution and differences between the services and officer grades.

It should be noted that the services generally use centralized competitive boards to select O-5s and O-6s for the residential SJSs and SSSs; the JCWS remains the primary venue for young field grade officers and individuals who are not selected for senior residential offerings (as is shown in Figure 4.7). For top talent personnel, there can be potential conflicts between gaining joint experiences and the services' preferred career timelines for officers. In a study based on qualitative interviews, Brian T. Watkins found that "[c]areer timelines are almost always an issue when considering joint assignment placement, and an officer's successful advancement still relies on performing well in service designated key developmental positions at each grade."[1] Accordingly, we expect the services to carefully manage the point in the career at which an officer gains joint experience.

Conversely, the services can create JQOs by allowing officers to achieve joint experience first and then to complete JPME-II via an SJS or SSS. Highly competitive officers for O-6 command or O-7 promotion often must complete PME at this senior level, providing the services with an opportunity to create a broad swath of JQOs at the same time that those officers are completing mandatory education. This method is not without costs, as the services delay the creation of JQOs until grade O-6 and thus suppress the inventory of JQOs. Furthermore, by delinking joint experience and joint education, many officers will complete a joint tour without having previously completed JPME-II. Accordingly, we will analyze differences that emerge by JPME-II institution and examine any differences between the services and officer grades.

---

[1] Brian T. Watkins, *Are We Too Dumb to Execute Our Own Doctrine? An Analysis of Professional Military Education, Talent Management, and Their Ability to Meet the Intent of the Capstone Concept for Joint Operations*, Norfolk, Va.: Joint Forces Staff College, Joint Advanced Warfighting School, 2016, p. 32.

JPME-II Sequencing with Joint Experience

Figure 5.1 shows the aggregated sequencing outcomes by JPME-II institutional type for all active component field grade officers with an S-JDA experiential tour who were designated as JQOs for the time period FY 2008 to FY 2017. Note that the JCWS is the only option available for officers to receive JPME-II during the course of their joint duty assignment. The JCWS is typically attended as a temporary duty assignment back to the school, located in Norfolk, Virginia, to complete the ten-week program of instruction. And due to recent policy changes, the JCWS also offers its JPME-II granting program in a few satellite locations that are in close proximity to CCMDs. Currently available JDAMIS data does not allow us to distinguish between these two JCWS offerings.

Of the JCWS program graduates who eventually were designated as JQOs, about equal portions completed the instruction either during (38 percent) or after (37 percent) their joint duty assignment, and the remaining 25 percent graduated before their assignment. The outcomes for the JCWS contrast to those of SJSs and SSSs, which are both residential educational programs that last upwards of ten months. Similarly, both of these longer programs require a permanent change of station. In the case of an SJS, approximately 60 percent of its graduates complete their degrees prior to their joint assignment. Conversely, 65 percent of SSS graduates who receive JPME-II credit do so after they have already finished their joint assignment.

When examining sequencing trends over fiscal years by service, as is shown in Figure 5.2, the Marine Corps is the only service that tends to send greater portions of its field grade officers to JPME-II prior to assignment. No service—except for the Marine Corps, in only three years—met the traditional expectation (as intended by the spirit of the GNA) that education prior to assignment should be the standard.

Figure 5.1
JPME-II Sequencing in Relation to S-JDA Tour, by Granting Institution

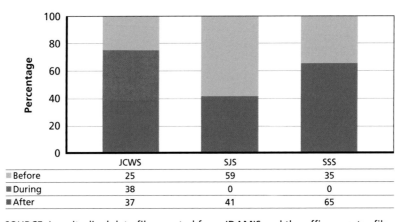

	JCWS	SJS	SSS
Before	25	59	35
During	38	0	0
After	37	41	65

SOURCE: Longitudinal data files created from JDAMIS and the officer master file.

Figure 5.2
JPME-II Sequencing in Relation to S-JDA Tour, by Fiscal Year and Service

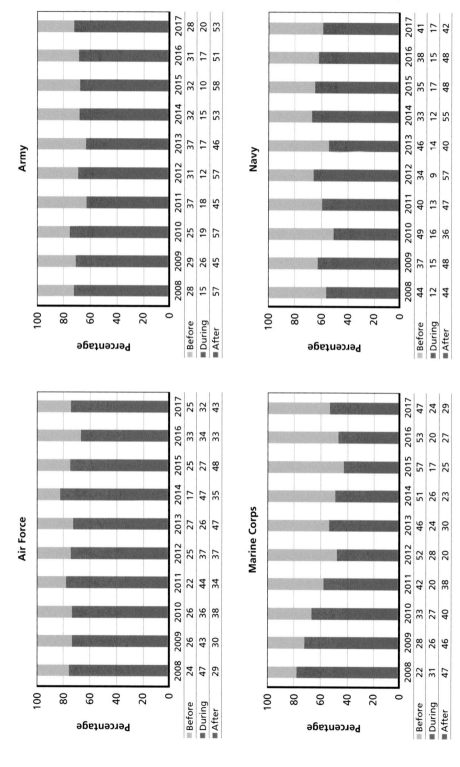

SOURCE: Longitudinal data files created from JDAMIS and the officer master file.

Conversely, the Army and the Navy have the highest percentages of JQOs who complete JPME-II after their assignment (with averages across the ten-year period of 52 percent and 46 percent, respectively). The Air Force had the largest percentage of officers completing their educational requirements during their joint assignments (with an average of 38 percent over the ten-year period, though this appears to be trending downward). These trends offer support to prior research that reported that combatant commanders raised concerns about the quality or abilities of the officers who were assigned to their staffs to successfully deal with joint matters.[2]

We looked deeper into these service findings to examine potential trends across pay grades, as is shown in Figure 5.3. For these results we collapsed across fiscal years to simplify the analysis and prevent overinterpretation of findings based on small cell sizes. Our findings show that only a small minority of O-4s attended JPME-II prior to an S-JDA tour. About one-fourth of O-4s attended JPME-II prior to an S-JDA tour in the Army or Navy, but 10 percent or less attended JPME-II prior to an S-JDA in the Air Force or Marine Corps. This is an interesting finding in that junior officers are most likely in greatest need of preparations in joint matters given their limited career histories and broadening assignments.

Completing JPME-II during an S-JDA tour is the most common sequencing option for producing an O-4 JQO. Corresponding to the relative dearth of O-4s who attend JPME-II prior to an S-JDA tour, the Air Force and Marine Corps have more O-4s attend JPME-II in the midst of an S-JDA than before or after that tour combined. At the O-5 level, completing JPME-II during an S-JDA tour is also a common sequence, though occurs less frequently than observed with O-4s.

The narrative changes when evaluating the sequence for O-6s. While O-4s will attend the JCWS exclusively, O-6s will be more likely to attend JPME-II through an SJS or SSS. In the Air Force and Navy, about one-half of O-6s complete JPME-II prior to an S-JDA tour; in the Marine Corps, nearly three-fourths complete JPME-II prior to an S-JDA tour. In contrast to the Marine Corps, Army statistics show nearly the opposite pattern: 76 percent complete JPME-II after an S-JDA tour. Very few O-6s, regardless of service, complete JPME-II during an S-JDA tour, which likely reflects that many O-6s will achieve JPME-II through an SJS or SSS or that they cannot "afford" to be away from their joint assignment due to the criticality of their responsibilities.

In aggregate, JPME-II infrequently occurs prior to an S-JDA tour. Only in the Marine Corps, and only in a few years, did a majority of officers attend JPME-II prior to an S-JDA tour. The decision to open up satellite campuses for the JCWS likely exacerbates the trend, mitigated only slightly by excluding JCWS classroom time from the length of the S-JDA tour. The historic ease by which an officer can attend the JCWS at the joint duty location decreases the necessity of a long temporary duty assignment and the high budgetary cost of attendance. But satellite JCWS locations do not fully

---

2   Fenty, 2008.

Figure 5.3
JPME-II Sequencing in Relation to S-JDA Tour, by Service and Grade

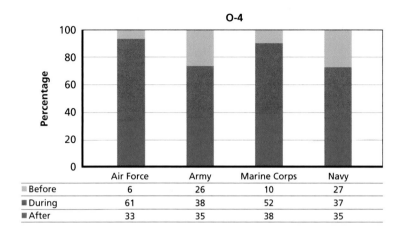

O-4

	Air Force	Army	Marine Corps	Navy
Before	6	26	10	27
During	61	38	52	37
After	33	35	38	35

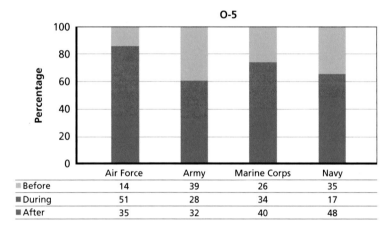

O-5

	Air Force	Army	Marine Corps	Navy
Before	14	39	26	35
During	51	28	34	17
After	35	32	40	48

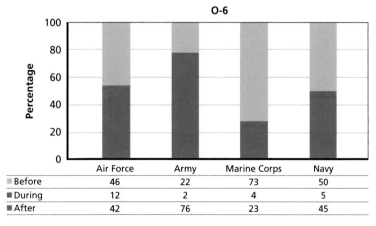

O-6

	Air Force	Army	Marine Corps	Navy
Before	46	22	73	50
During	12	2	4	5
After	42	76	23	45

SOURCE: Longitudinal data files created from JDAMIS and the officer
master file.

explain the trend. The relative popularity of JPME-II during an S-JDA tour showed wide variance before the first satellite location was established in FY 2012, and the pattern of behavior has not substantially changed in the years since then.

Figure 5.4 shows JPME-II sequencing by service and granting institution. Compared to the other services, the Air Force makes greatest use of JCWS attendance while officers are in their S-JDA assignments (54 percent), followed by the Marine Corps at 43 percent. Notably, the Marine Corps sends essentially all of its SJS attendees to complete JPME-II prior to the officers' assignments (94 percent). The Air Force is the next closest service, at 68 percent, while the Army only has 35 percent of its JQOs attend an SJS prior to their joint assignments. Similarly, the Army has only 11 percent of its SSS graduates complete their JPME-II prior to joint assignments. The Air Force is not quite to this extreme but has only 33 percent of its SSS graduates complete joint education prior to their joint duty.

Figure 5.5 shows that the trends of Figure 5.4 are only intensified when considering grade. Junior grades tend to attend the JCWS during their joint tour. All Marine Corps O-6s and 70 percent of O-5s attend an SJS prior to their joint assignment. All O-5s in the Air Force and Army attend an SSS after their joint duty. The same is essentially true for Air Force and Army O-6s: 57 percent and 88 percent, respectively, attend an SSS after their joint assignment.

As is shown in Figure 5.1, the services have a tendency to schedule officers' S-JDA prior to JPME-II instruction for any institution other than an SJS. As follow-on analysis showed, this trend is accentuated when comparisons are made by service and/or grade. Given that the intention of the GNA was to have experienced officers in joint matters (e.g., a synergy between education and assignments) and the current sequencing of S-JDA, we decided to characterize the distribution of time between JPME-II graduation and JQO appointment.

Time Between Education and Joint Qualified Officer Appointment

Table 5.1 shows the distributions of time in months between JPME-II graduation and JQO appointment for officers who completed JPME-II either before or after their S-JDA completion. (All durations include time associated with processing the JQO application through the service and Joint Staff and gaining the Secretary of Defense's approval.) As expected, the "JPME-II before" distribution was much longer, as it included the duration of the S-JDA. In theory, this time frame can extend upwards of 36 months, but in practice it varies by service, grade, and granting institution. Although some differences may be statistically significant, from a practical standpoint the median differences reflect only a month or so over the course of an entire military career.

Figure 5.4
JPME-II Sequencing in Relation to S-JDA Tour, by Service and Granting Institution

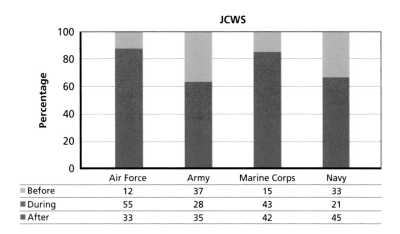

JCWS

	Air Force	Army	Marine Corps	Navy
■ Before	12	37	15	33
■ During	55	28	43	21
■ After	33	35	42	45

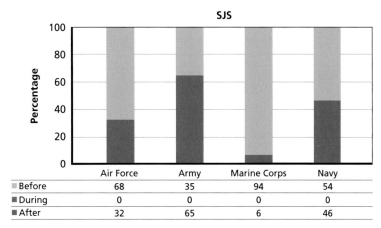

SJS

	Air Force	Army	Marine Corps	Navy
■ Before	68	35	94	54
■ During	0	0	0	0
■ After	32	65	6	46

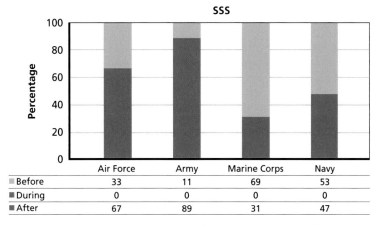

SSS

	Air Force	Army	Marine Corps	Navy
■ Before	33	11	69	53
■ During	0	0	0	0
■ After	67	89	31	47

SOURCE: Longitudinal data files created from JDAMIS and the officer master file.

Figure 5.5
JPME-II Sequencing in Relation to S-JDA Tour, by Service, Grade, and Granting Institution

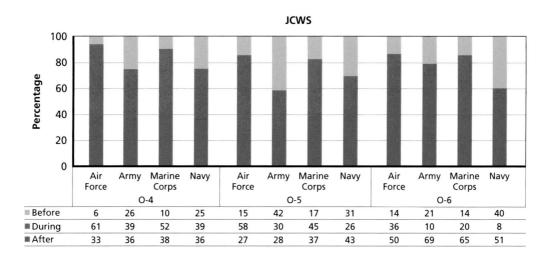

JCWS

	Air Force	Army	Marine Corps	Navy	Air Force	Army	Marine Corps	Navy	Air Force	Army	Marine Corps	Navy
			O-4				O-5				O-6	
▪ Before	6	26	10	25	15	42	17	31	14	21	14	40
▪ During	61	39	52	39	58	30	45	26	36	10	20	8
▪ After	33	36	38	36	27	28	37	43	50	69	65	51

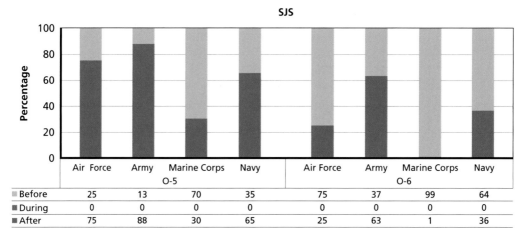

SJS

	Air Force	Army	Marine Corps	Navy	Air Force	Army	Marine Corps	Navy
			O-5				O-6	
▪ Before	25	13	70	35	75	37	99	64
▪ During	0	0	0	0	0	0	0	0
▪ After	75	88	30	65	25	63	1	36

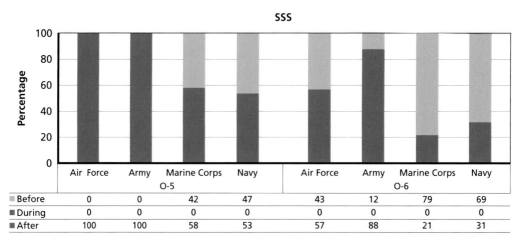

SSS

	Air Force	Army	Marine Corps	Navy	Air Force	Army	Marine Corps	Navy
			O-5				O-6	
▪ Before	0	0	42	47	43	12	79	69
▪ During	0	0	0	0	0	0	0	0
▪ After	100	100	58	53	57	88	21	31

Table 5.1
Time between JPME-II Graduation and Joint Qualified Officer Appointment

	Category	Rank Order Within Category	N	Months		
				25th Percentile	Median	75th Percentile
Total sample			7,592	3.4	10.5	36.7
JPME-II before			3,264	30.3	37.9	42.7
JPME-II after			4,328	2.5	4.0	7.0
JPME-II before	Air Force	2	888	28.6	36.1	40.8
	Army	4	905	35.2	38.9	42.6
	Marine Corps	1	493	28.3	35.7	39.3
	Navy	3	978	31.0	38.0	55.9
JPME-II after	Air Force	4	1,311	3.0	4.7	8.6
	Army	1	1,539	1.8	2.9	7.0
	Marine Corps	3	365	2.4	4.3	7.0
	Navy	2	1,113	3.0	3.6	5.5
JPME-II before	O-4	2	154	33.5	38.0	40.2
	O-5	2	1,359	32.9	38.0	41.1
	O-6	1	1,751	28.9	37.7	43.4
JPME-II after	O-4	3	381	3.0	4.6	7.5
	O-5	2	1,835	2.9	4.1	7.0
	O-6	1	2,112	2.0	3.6	7.0
JPME-II before	JCWS	3	1,593	33.9	38.2	42.7
	SJS	1	1,048	28.5	36.8	42.3
	SSS	2	623	29.0	37.4	40.0
JPME-II after	JCWS	2	2,416	2.7	4.3	7.3
	SJS	1	734	2.0	3.5	4.9
	SSS	1	1,178	2.0	3.3	7.1

SOURCE: Longitudinal data files created from JDAMIS and the officer master file.

NOTE: Total sample excludes individuals who completed JPME-II during their S-JDA but does include all field grade officers across the period FY 2008 to FY 2017 who have completed JPME-II, an S-JDA assignment, and have been designated a JQO. Rank order within category is based on median months (shortest to longest) separately for JPME-II before and after for each of the categorical variables.

Given the emphasis that the Marine Corps places on its officers receiving JPME prior to their joint assignments, it is consistent that the Marine Corps has the least median duration between JPME-II graduation and JQO appointment. The Air Force is about as equally efficient when JPME-II occurs before a joint assignment. Conversely in cases where JPME-II is completed after an assignment, the Army is considerably faster in accomplishing JQO appointments for its officers.

When examining grade differences, O-6s are consistently processed faster than either O-5s or O-4s. This is true whether JPME-II is completed before or after joint assignments.

For the different types of joint educational institution, graduates from SJSs and SSSs are quite similar for the median time between their JPME-II graduation and JQO appointment both before and after joint assignments. However, graduates from the JCWS take consistently longer to achieve their JQO designation.

Considering Joint Waivers

Due to the complexities of service and joint officer management policies, as well as the needs of the services and joint organizations, it is inherent that any process will need to have exceptions or waivers to standing policies. The joint education and officer management processes have a range of possible waivers that require increasing levels of approval—to include authorization by the CJSC or Secretary of Defense. The use of waivers is intended to be for exceptional circumstances only, as indicated by the required approval levels.

Unfortunately, waiver information collected within JDAMIS is inconsistent in many respects: it is inconsistent over time, not reflective of policy changes, and not well documented in terms of data specifications. The one exception appears to be waivers associated with tour length curtailment. Such waivers can be requested by the services for officers in critical occupational specialties who are in line for (or need service education) for command positions. Therefore, this was the only waiver information that we analyzed.

Table 5.2 highlights the trends for tour length curtailment waivers through a number of characteristics: fiscal year, grade, and service. Waivers are expressed as a percentage of the respective variable population (e.g., all field grade JQOs are considered separately by grade and service). Such waivers are very consistent over time. Over the ten-year period of analysis, the percentage of waivers has had limited variability, at around 10 percent annually. As would be expected, these waivers are used in greater number and portion for higher grades because of the higher numbers of officers who are going into command assignments. Compared to the other services, the Air Force and Army make greatest use of this waiver, at 13 percent and 12 percent, respectively.

Table 5.2
S-JDA Tour Length Curtailment Waiver Trends

Fiscal Year	2008	2009	2010	2011	2012	2013	2014	2015	2016	2017	Total
Waivers granted	81	113	116	141	89	131	75	94	90	65	1,045
FY inventory	938	1,027	1,555	1,116	856	1,089	900	916	910	714	10,021
Annual percentage	9%	11%	11%	13%	10%	12%	8%	10%	10%	9%	10%

Grade	O-4		O-5		O-6		Total
Waivers granted	48		361		636		1,045
Grade inventory	1,085		4,818		4,118		10,021
Grade percentage	4%		7%		15%		10%

Service	Air Force	Army	Marine Corps	Navy	Total
Waivers granted	460	359	53	173	1,045
Service inventory	3,523	2,948	1,128	2,422	10,021
Service percentage	13%	12%	5%	7%	10%

SOURCE: Longitudinal data files created from JDAMIS and the officer master file.

NOTE: Analysis is based on individuals granted waivers relative to their respective populations based on field grade officers across FY 2008 to FY 2017 who have completed JPME-II and an S-JDA assignment and have been designated a JQO.

CHAPTER SIX

Joint Qualified Officer Designation Experiences: Two Case Studies

Considering historical trends provides an understanding of the typical or due-course approach to achieving JQO designation. It is also informative to examine the paths of individuals who have successfully navigated the processes in becoming senior leaders. As a first case study, we examined a recent cohort of Army brigadier generals to see how their experiences compare with the previous trend analysis. Individuals make career determining decisions at multiple points in their career but the grade of O-5s is particularly critical as officers weigh their personal and family situations versus the likelihood of future military promotion and continued success. Therefore, we considered a second case study of O-5s that contrasts officers who were designated as JQOs across all services and whether they were or were not promoted to O-6.

Senior Officer Experience: Army Brigadier Generals

In the first case study we examined the pathways through which Army brigadier generals (O-7s) received their qualification as JQOs. The biographies of Army general officers are public information and contain information on PME, assignment history, joint experience, operational experience, and awards and decorations. We excluded from our analysis Army O-7s in the academy professor, acquisition, chaplain, medical, and judge advocate fields, as officers in those career fields may receive a waiver for joint experience for promotion to O-7.[1] Based on biographies accessed in July 2018, 116 Army O-7s are included in our case study.

The biographies contain a listing of substantial PME, including educational experiences that award JPME-II credit. As is noted in Table 6.1, some officers received education from more than one institution; eight officers attended both the JCWS and an SSS. From the biographies, we cannot tell whether an officer received JQO status from one or the other JPME-II experience. Three officers had no JPME-II education

---

[1]   Waivers for JQO status for promotion to O-7 are listed in the biographies. Some officers in these categories required waivers, but some did not. For consistency in analysis, we excluded all officers from these career fields.

Table 6.1
JPME-II Granting Institutions for Case Study of Recent Army O-7s

JPME-II Granting Institution	N	%
Senior service school	36	31%
Senior joint school	34	29%
JCWS	35	30%
Multiple institutions	8	7%
Unknown/missing	3	3%
Total	116	100%

SOURCE: U.S. Army General Officer Management Office, Army Brigadier General (O-7) Public Resumes, 2018.
NOTE: Analysis excludes Army O-7s in the academy professor, acquisition, chaplain, medical, and judge advocate fields.

listed on their biographies and therefore they received waivers, or completed multiple joint duty assignment tours, or the data were inadvertently omitted (which is unlikely given the standard reporting requirements for general or flag officers).

Keen observers may note that the number of Army O-7s who graduated from an SSS is less than the total number of Army O-7s; such education is typically thought to be a prerequisite for generalship consideration. All Army O-7s complete an educational experience at the SSS level, but many Army O-7s will complete an SSS fellowship in lieu of attending a traditional SSS.[2] For instance, for the academic year 2012–2013 (a period when several current Army O-7s attended an SSS), the Army offered 39 SSS fellowships at various think tanks, research institutes, and universities. Examples include the Center for a New American Security, Harvard University, the Institute for Defense Analyses, the Massachusetts Institute of Technology, Stanford University, and the U.S. Institute of Peace. Within that academic year the Army planned for 213 Army students at SSSs, 93 Army students at SJSs, 65 Army students at fellowships, and nine Army students at senior foreign schools.[3] Because an SSS fellowship will not grant JPME-II, officers must have completed coursework at the JCWS at some point in their career to meet the education requirement for JQO status.

---

[2]   Other services use similar programs, albeit in service-specific language. Air Force Instruction 36-2301 Attachment 4, "Air Force Officer / Civilian SDE Fellowship (AFF) Program Descriptions," 2010, pp. 59–60, lists 26 fellowship programs that qualify for senior developmental education credit. According to Army Regulation 350-1, Army Training and Leader Development, 2017, p. 84, Army officers participating in a fellowship "forgo any other opportunity for SSC education."

[3]   The precise allocation of seats at various institutions and programs will vary from year to year. Information on the academic year 2012–2013 program overviews and seat allocations can be found in U.S. Army Combined Arms Center, *Senior Service College / Fellowship / Foreign School Information, AY 2012–2013*. Fort Leavenworth, Kan.: U.S. Army Combined Arms Center, 2012.

Table 6.2
Comparison of Senior Educational Experiences for Case Study of Recent Army O-7s

Basis for Educational Experience	Background Experiences of Army O-7s		Allocated SSS Equivalent Slots in Academic Year 2012–2013	
	N	%	N	%
Senior service school	45	39%	213	56%
Senior joint school	38	33%	93	24%
Senior foreign school	1	1%	9	2%
Fellowship	32	27%	65	17%
Total	116	100%	380	99%

SOURCES: U.S. Army General Officer Management Office, 2018.
NOTE: Analysis excludes Army O-7s in the academy professor, acquisition, chaplain, medical, and judge advocate fields. Percentage may not sum to 100 percent due to rounding.

As is shown in Table 6.2, we compared the relative portions of background educa-tion for the case study of individuals who have achieved O-7 to the relative allocation percentages (and thereby funding) for slots allocated to various education opportuni-ties in academic year 2012–13. If this academic year can be viewed as typical, it is interesting to note that a higher portion of Army officers promoted to O-7 completed fellowship and SJS programs than the allocation of those programs among all educa-tion opportunities. Twenty-seven percent of O-7s completed fellowships, while only 17 percent of all education slots were fellowships; and 33 percent of O-7s completed senior joint schooling, versus 24 percent of education slots that were in SJSs.

The Army O-7 biographies list joint experiences, including the unit of assign-ment, location, and duration. From this information we determined the likely experi-ential pathway through which the officers attained JQO status (E-JDA versus S-JDA). The biographies do not list whether the joint experience qualified as an E-JDA tour or an S-JDA tout, but our knowledge of qualification standards allowed us to make educated guesses. Joint experiences of less than 15 months and occurring in an HFP/IDP location clearly deserve categorization as an E-JDA tour; 27 months on the Joint Staff qualifies as an S-JDA tour. Between those archetypes, we used our judgment to categorize the pathway to JQO and recognize that our findings are subject to some measurement error. Table 6.3 shows that Army O-7s are almost equally likely to have reached JQO status through the E-JDA pathway as through the S-JDA.

We see substantial differences between the Army O-7s in this case study and the larger population of field grade officers, discussed in Chapter Three, in which a majority of JQO field grade officers received JPME-II through the JCWS, with much smaller percentages from SJSs or SSSs (see Table 3.2). Likewise, Army O-7 biographies tell a different story regarding joint experience, with roughly equal percentages coming from each joint duty assignment pathway. While the S-JDA pathway is much more

Table 6.3
Likely Experiential Path to Joint Qualified Officer for Case Study of Recent Army O-7s

Likely Experiential Path	N	%
E-JDA	55	47%
S-JDA	61	53%
Total	116	100%

SOURCES: U.S. Army General Officer Management Office, 2018.
NOTE: Analysis excludes Army O-7s in the academy professor, acquisition, chaplain, medical, and judge advocate fields. Biographies do not list joint experiential path taken, so we made informed decisions based primarily on duration of joint experience and location of assignment.

common among the larger field grade population, the E-JDA and S-JDA pathway portions are much closer among Army O-7s.

We suspect that many reasons exist for the observed differences. Those who rise to the rank of Army O-7 may react to career time constraints differently than will lower ranked peers, most of whom will not attain the rank of O-7. Prospective Army O-7s may be more diligent or persuasive in E-JDA applications than the larger field grade population. Though SJSs make up a small percentage of those who reach JQO status, a substantial percentage of their graduates may attain the rank of O-7.

Promotion Outcomes: O-5s

In a second case study we examined the promotion outcomes of O-5 JQOs. Service preferences influence the career timing of JQO production, with some services creating JQOs in greater numbers earlier in officer careers. We evaluated whether an O-5 JQO was promoted to O-6 within seven years of promotion to O-5. We chose the seven-year cutoff to capture the window during which an O-5 could be promoted to O-6. Similarly, we tracked the same metrics for non-JQOs to serve as a means of comparison. Table 6.4 shows the promotion outcomes. We found that only 28 JQOs were promoted to O-6 after the seven-year point, which suggests that this period is reasonable.

More O-5 JQOs are promoted to O-6 than not promoted across all four services. For every O-5 JQO not promoted to O-6, 1.9 O-5 JQOs were promoted to O-6 in the Air Force and Navy. That ratio declines to 1.5 for the Army and further declines to 1.4 in the Marine Corps. The Army and Marine Corps arrived at that situation in entirely different ways, however. Recall that in Figure 3.10, the Marine Corps led the services in the percentage of O-5s who were JQOs, while the Army had the lowest percentage among the services. The Marine Corps selected a lower percentage of its JQOs for

Table 6.4
Promotion Outcomes for O-5 Joint Qualified Officers

Service	Promoted Within Seven Years	Not Promoted	Ratio of Promoted to Not Promoted	Not Promoted or Separated	Ratio of Promoted to Not Promoted or Separated	Not Considered
Air Force						
JQO	650	344	1.9	756	0.9	523
Non-JQO	5,001	3,287	1.5	9,640	0.5	8,371
Army						
JQO	578	384	1.5	770	0.8	480
Non-JQO	5,666	3,202	1.8	9,578	0.6	7,451
Marine Corps						
JQO	165	122	1.4	204	0.8	157
Non-JQO	739	597	1.2	1,898	0.4	1,534
Navy						
JQO	615	326	1.9	493	1.2	444
Non-JQO	3,480	2,657	1.3	5,546	0.6	5,259
Total	16,894	10,919	1.5	28,885	0.6	24,219
JQO	2,008	1,176	1.7	2,223	0.9	1,604
Non-JQO	14,886	9,743	1.5	26,662	0.5	22,615

NOTE: An O-5 JQO with less than 7 years' time in the grade, not promoted to O-6, and not separated from the military is reflected in the "Not Considered" column. For instance, an O-5 JQO who is still in the military with a date of rank in 2015 would be in that category.

promotion to O-6, but started with a greater percentage of the eligible population as JQOs. The Army, conversely, started with the smallest percentage of the eligible population as JQOs, and selected a lower percentage of them for promotion than the Air Force or Navy. As Figure 3.9 shows, the Army produces many more JQOs at O-6 than the other services, suggesting that earlier JQO designation in a career does not carry the same weight as it does in the other services.

For three of the four services, the ratio of JQOs promoted to O-6 is greater than the ratio of non-JQOs promoted to O-6. This suggests that JQO designation is associated with improved probability of selection to O-6, though one cannot assign causality to JQO designation. Those designated as JQOs may differ from their non-JQO peers in ways beyond their joint experience and joint education. The Army's experience reverses the trend, as non-JQOs are promoted at a higher rate than JQOs. For the Army, officers designated as JQOs are less likely to be promoted to O-6 compared with non-JQO peers.[4] We cannot tell from the available data if the Army traditionally values other assignments more than joint assignments in terms of promotion decisions, if Army officers receive less advantageous performance evaluations in joint assignments than in Army assignments, or if officers achieving JQO designation before the O-6 board started with fewer quality markers before even achieving JQO designation. This trend for the Army is not observed when also including "Separated" along with "Not Promoted." In other words, the ratios show that Army rates for O-6 promotion and remaining in service are somewhat better when the officer is a JQO compared with not being a JQO.

Evaluating promotion outcomes for senior officers is always confounded by retirement decisions. Most officers will reach twenty years of service before consideration for O-6. Officers might know the likelihood of promotion to O-6 based on the strength of their performance record; less competitive officers may retire at a greater rate than those who believe they possess more competitive files.

Table 6.4 also shows the ratio of O-5 JQOs promoted to O-6 within seven years to those who were either not promoted within seven years or separated from the military. For three of the four services, the ratio is less than one. For the Navy, however, the ratio is greater than one, indicating that an O-5 JQO in the Navy is more likely to be selected for O-6 than to either not be selected for promotion or to separate from the Navy. The ratio of JQOs selected for promotion is greater than the ratio of non-JQO peers for all four services.

JQO designation appears to be a favorable characteristic in three of four services for O-5s under promotion consideration for O-6, at least for officers who go before an O-6 board. The Army, which creates more JQOs at the O-6 grade, promotes a smaller percentage of JQOs than non-JQOs. For those services where JQO designation improves promotion selection, we cannot determine from the available data if this is because the services engage in talent management by ensuring JQO designation for those most competitive for O-6 or if the JQO designation in and of itself increases the competitiveness of an officer's performance file. Any analysis of promotion outcomes must also consider those who separated from the military, but we cannot determine if those who separated are the "shadow denominator" when determining a true promotion rate for JQOs.[5]

---

[4] Our data aggregates promotion outcomes across all competitive categories in a military service. Officers compete for promotion by competitive category. Results within competitive categories may differ substantially.

[5] In the simplest terms, a promotion rate is calculated by dividing the number selected for promotion by the number considered for promotion. Those who separate from the service before consideration for promotion reduce the denominator of that equation, in turn inflating the promotion rate.

CHAPTER SEVEN

Observations and Implications

Prior chapters presented the results or trends of how the services have produced JQOs over time and how those trends vary by certain policy-relevant characteristics. Such trends are merely descriptive of historical outcomes and do not necessarily reflect what may happen in the future. Similarly, trends do not necessarily result in or directly lead to recommendations; a broader context is needed within which to interpret such outcomes and draw inferences.

To gain a greater context for these trends and to appreciate possible factors that contributed to their variances, we reached out to the JOM and JPME offices of the military services, Joint Staff, and OSD. During the course of these engagements we sought to understand their perceptions on the validity of the data presented, their historical recollection of policy and operational events that could have affected JQO findings, thoughts on the implications of the JQO findings, and potential JOM and JPME practices that they perceived have been effective or could benefit others. This chapter captures the themes associated with these discussions. We greatly benefited from the insights, experiences, and perspectives of the various agencies.

There Is a Need for Authoritative Data and a Comparison Baseline

The Benefits of Quality Data

As discussed in Chapter 1, JDAMIS is the primary system used by the services and Joint Staff to manage the JQO production process. All service, Joint Staff, and OSD stakeholders acknowledged the value of JDAMIS but also its limitations and lamented the need for a more accurate and authoritative information source to support individual officers in personal career choices and decisionmakers as they seek to develop, assess, and refine appropriate and responsive policies.

This report focuses exclusively on JQO supply—tracking the basic elements of jointness starting at the earliest developmental stages of officers' careers to their potential consideration for promotion to general or flag officer. We did not examine the demand for JQOs due to even greater inconsistency of information about the positions that form the JDAL. Improving the accuracy of this demand information should be the focus of future analysis to supplement these JQO supply trends. OSD is in the process of procuring system enhancements and updates to the JDAMIS business processes and software. Close coordination and feedback from the JOM and JPME stakeholders will be essential throughout the system improvement process to ensure that their past difficulties and future information needs are sufficiently addressed.

The Benefits of Considering Trends

Historically, the services, Congress, Joint Staff, and OSD have viewed annual reports that detail fiscal year JOM and JPME results. Initially these annual reports were prepared for Congress, but that requirement has now changed so that OSD is the primary recipient. The reporting elements have also changed, with comparability of promotion rates for joint and service headquarters officers no longer being conveyed to Congress. These annual reports offered a limited view of the JQO process by providing only a snapshot of a single year. As a result, there is no basis for assessing the meaning of such results in terms of either magnitude or consistency.

During our conversations with the services and Joint Staff, all parties recognized the value of a multiyear perspective. The data and methods employed in this report provide a consistent analytical basis for defining variables, describing concepts, and calculating trends. Using our results, each service was able to spot and assess the nuances and even impacts of its past policy initiatives. Not all such initiatives were formalized in official policies or regulations; many reflected more subtle leadership guidance, prioritization, or intent. Therefore, a longer-term outlook allowed subject matter experts to perceive effects that were not readily apparent from a single-year snapshot. Such a long view also allowed stakeholders to account for the natural lags in policies taking effect and their outcomes being realized.

The subject matter experts also valued the comparisons of JQO trends across services, which highlighted cultural differences, and they were interested in determining what potential policy details or implementation dynamics may have benefit for their respective service.

The Benefits of Establishing a Baseline

Finally, the services desired a common historical baseline to assist their efforts in determining and assessing the future impact of policy changes. Specifically, they understood the considerable number and magnitude of policy adjustments implemented with the revision of DoDI 1300.19. This significant policy revision highlights a number of questions for future trend analysis and research issues:

- What are the overall and detailed effects associated with the shortening of tour lengths for standard joint duty assignment from 36 to 24 months? How quickly will the services transition to this new minimum? Will this transition be differentially used across grades and occupational types?

- Do the same issues and questions also apply to the reduction in points necessary for an experiential joint duty assignment?
- Will there be an effect on the overall quality of joint officers resulting from shorter tour lengths or accumulation of fewer joint points? Is 24 months and 24 points sufficient experience for a JQO? Do the findings vary by grade?

The services desired both a common and historical basis to consistently evaluate such questions in a standardized manner both within and across their respective organizations. This was true for both the April 2018 policy changes and any additional future revisions.

Joint Qualified Officer Production Is Stable But May Be Declining

The Recently Constant Supply of Joint Qualified Officers Against Uncertain Demand

The trends over the last ten years show that all services have achieved considerable growth in absolute numbers for the inventory of field grade, active component JQOs (see Figure 3.1). However, during the FY 2015 to FY 2017 time frame, these numbers have stabilized in terms of actual inventory and even declined in terms of annual appointees (Figures 3.1 and 3.3). Given the limited time period of the declines, it is not discernable if they represent a trend or a random occurrence. However, these declines, observed across all services except the Marine Corps (which was constant), raise the question of whether there is sufficient supply to meet the demand for JQOs; that is an issue beyond the scope of the current study. Have the services now achieved JQO supply production totals that are equal to or are sufficient to satisfy the JQO demands of joint customers?

The Joint Staff conducts periodic and systematic validations of joint duty assignments that should provide further insight into this critical question. Therefore, a possible decline in JQO production may not be an issue if JQO demand is being sufficiently met. In a strict sense, individuals are designated as JQOs for only two reasons: (1) to fill critical JDAL positions (currently there are between 300 and 350 such positions across all grades), and (2) to qualify O-6s for general or flag officer promotion consideration (as a rough order of magnitude, less than 140 active component O-6s are promoted to O-7 on an annual basis across all services). If these are the only two demand requirements for JQOs (notwithstanding that others have argued that the total JDAL is representative of greater JQO demand), then annual JQO production numbers can surely meet demand, defined in this limited manner. Several services also thought that with reductions in their respective end strengths should be a commensurate reduction in joint duty assignment requirements. Such questions are the intended focus and purpose of the Joint Staff's periodic JDAL review and validation.

Increasing the Competitive Pool for General or Flag Officer Selection

JQO production has varied by service. While joint billets are distributed somewhat equally across military departments, a good number of joint positions are competitively sourced. The Army and Marine Corps have increased the percentage of JQOs in their officer corps over time (see Figure 3.2). However, the Air Force has the largest absolute number of JQOs (see Figure 3.1). Consideration of the relative differences with regard to number versus percentage of JQOs may reflect how the services manage and develop their officer corps in the intricate balance of officer quality in satisfying both service and joint assignment requirements. The net outcome will be officers who are able to effectively conduct and lead both service and joint operations, as well as individuals who will be competitive for selection to advantageous joint assignments and ultimately for the more coveted general and flag officer joint positions. From other work, we know that the majority of general and flag officers are tactical operations officers.[1] Therefore, we would expect the services to produce more JQOs in tactical operations than in other career fields to be competitive for senior joint leadership positions. This absolute JQO production hypothesis was observed only in the Marine Corps and Navy (Figure 3.7).[2]

Joint Task Force Capability Differences Across the Services Affect Experiential Path Utilization

The trend data show that the E-JDA experience path was increasingly used to achieve the JQO experiential requirement, and especially used by the Army. JDAMIS data did not allow for careful examination of JTF assignments, and it was through interviews and inference that we determined that the Army had greater recurring JTF requirements compared with the other services. This disparity contributes to the Army's high E-JDA utilization. Thereby, its officers' E-JDA application packages are validated at higher rates given that they likely served in more senior JTF positions that were concentrated in joint matters at the strategic level. Individual service augmentees are less likely to serve in either senior or strategic joint positions. Accordingly, tactical operations officers may have an advantage in E-JDA applications for operational deployment assignments than nontactical operations officers, even when serving in the same unit. Tactical operations officers may be unit commanders and can thus make a compelling case that the position meets the definition of joint matters. Conversely, nontactical

---

[1] RAND Corporation, *Realigning the Stars: A Methodology for Reviewing Active Component General and Flag Officer Requirements*, Santa Monica, Calif.: RAND Corporation, RR-2384-OSD, 2018.

[2] For instance, if half of general and flag officers come from tactical-operations (conservative estimate) and the services want a three to one ratio between qualified candidates and eventual general and flag officer selectees, then we should expect a much greater percentage of tactical operations officers as JQOs given that these officers are a minority in most services. Significant ratios between tactical operations to nontactical operations JQOs were only observed in the Navy, not the other services.

operations officers are more likely to serve in supporting roles and may have a harder time meeting the joint matters threshold.

Possible Explanations for Service Differences in Joint Qualified Officer Trends

It is evident that the services take diverse approaches to talent management and the timing associated with gaining joint experience. For example, the Air Force develops and maintains consistently large JQO inventories composed of officers early in their careers (as O-4s and O-5s) (see Figures 3.10 and 3.11). This outcome stands in stark contrast to other services. We learned through interviews that the Air Force is particularly focused on the early identification of "high potential" officers. Among other qualities, the Air Force tends to use selection into joint responsibilities, performance during joint education and assignments, and accomplishment of JQO designation as continued indicators of successful performance. Such trends may also reflect service differences in overall management of officer assignments: priority, timing, duration, and possible trade-offs of career-enhancing benefits for service versus joint assignments. It may be the case that the services are attempting to delay "time away" from military service at critical junctures or career points or simply postponing joint assignments as long as possible.

Another particularly striking finding is that the percentages of O-6s JQOs have increased considerably over time within each service. The trend is especially true for the Marine Corps: over 70 percent of its O-6s are JQOs. One interpretation of this trend is that JQO status as an O-6 has now become an established norm in an officer's career, in much the same way that earning a master's degree has become standard. As a range of policy modifications have made additional pathways to JQO available (e.g., E-JDA and JPME-II at SSSs), reasons for not being designated a JQO have become less defensible.

These observed trends could be influenced by or the result of differential service deployments over the last decade and the challenges to fully develop individuals not only as leaders but in the full scope of service warfighting requirements. Based on the limited data available, we were not able to determine if such deployments had a positive influence on JQO designation (through the E-JDA path) or were a hindrance given the time associated with operations that were not strategically oriented toward joint matters.

Finally, the trends could result from an interplay of all such factors. It is difficult to uniquely tease out these various factors associated with differing and evolving service philosophies concerning jointness, the complexity associated with individual officers' decisions and circumstances, and the effective management of personnel systems to address dynamic joint operational requirements.

Complexities in Interpreting Joint Personnel Policy Trends

As the previous chapters have illustrated, the services simultaneously manage multiple constraints as they seek to develop and employ officers who are proficient in joint matters. The maturity and acceptance of joint operational concepts have progressed considerably, yet personnel management has not kept pace.[3] Achieving service equities concurrently with desirable joint results is further complicated by the perspectives and set career length of individual officers. Likewise, policies that detail personnel management are not always sufficiently specified nor are expected outcomes adequately detailed and captured in terms of accurate measurements.

Trend analysis seeks to overcome such difficulties by focusing on observable after-effects following sufficient time and replications. However, the interpretation of trends can be complex as one seeks to infer initial policy intentions, account for inconsistent policy implementations, overcome imperfect causal relationships, and project future implications. The net results can be conflicting or competing interpretations. The work documented in this report is no different.

Past personnel policy changes have been an attempt to better reflect the realities of joint operational demands and provide greater flexibility to accommodate service needs. At times these two objectives can be diametrically opposed or raise further questions for exploration. Examples include the following:

- The implementation of the joint qualification system resulted in the creation of the E-JDA path, which sought credit for joint experiences by constructing equivalencies or alternatives to full joint duty tours. The trends showed increased use of E-JDAs, especially for services with greater strategic joint deployment responsibilities. It is an open question as to the quality and equivalency of JQOs designated by either the E-JDA or S-JDA paths.
- Reduced tour durations (from 36 to 24 months) and corresponding reductions in joint qualification points were requested by the services as they argued that their command tours were typically two years. These revisions have yet to be implemented long enough to determine their impact on joint outcomes.
- Joint education in the form of JPME-II is no longer a prerequisite in an officer's preparation for a joint assignment but rather a matter of timing and availability determined by the services. It is the perspective of and assessment by the joint community that is missing from this calculus. Are officers reporting to their assignments sufficiently prepared and capable of performing their joint billet responsibilities?
- All SSSs are now accredited to provide JPME-II. An unintended outcome of this expansion is that the services are explicitly waiting until later in officers' careers to achieve both senior service education and senior joint education simultaneously.

---

[3]   Thie, Harrell, Yardley, Oshiro, Potter, Schirmer, and Lim, 2005.

This results in many officers relying on JPME-I as the only joint preparations for their joint duty assignment and the later awarding of JQO designations at higher grades.

- Based on shorter durations, more annual convenings, and greater geographical dispersion of the JCWS JPME-II program, the services made consistent and high utilization of this educational offering, to even include higher grades. The services were not able to address the question of equivalency of graduate outcomes compared with SJSs or SSSs other than all programs generated the same status as regarded graduates.
- The trend analysis has shown that JQO designations are coming at higher grades or later in officers' careers. This trend is a paradox, as the preponderance of joint duty assignments is for O-4s and junior O-5s. In combination with joint education also being received later in officers' careers, the conundrum is whether the officers being assigned to the joint community are being fully prepared for the rigors of their joint assignments. The policy to examine and report equity of promotion rates of joint officers versus officers assigned to service headquarters is no longer a requirement and should possibly be reconsidered given these discrepancies.
- Another interpretation of the significant and continuing increase of O-6s JQOs is that all services are strictly adhering to the legislative requirements that all officers must be so designated prior to being considered for promotion to general or flag officer. Such explicit and well-defined policy requirements appear to effectively influence service officer management behaviors.
- As the services continue to face evolving threats, the need for more advanced joint operational concepts continues to grow, and thus so does the demand for even more joint warfighters. Jointness is progressing beyond interservice capability to also include interagency, multinational, and coalition jointness for an ever expanding set of mission areas—both in space and in cyberwarfare. The existing constraints will remain, and they will play an even greater role in the development and management of joint personnel.

The fundamental question in each of these areas is the extent to which policy changes are contributing to or detracting from the ultimate objective of providing sufficient numbers and quality of joint officers. The Joint Staff and OSD—through the specification of required service metrics, annual report submissions, educational institution accreditation processes, and periodic engagements with combatant commanders—should work to assess the net outcome of policy changes on the quality of JQOs and their ability to satisfy the performance expectations of the joint community. Until such time, trend analysis can lead to a proper, albeit incomplete, discussion, vetting, and assessment of policy changes.

Joint Education Is Accomplished Based on Timing and Availability

Considerations for JPME-II Granting Institution Offerings

With JPME policy changes that allowed both SJSs and SSSs to confer JPME-II graduation status, there are now a wide variety of venues from which to complete joint educational requirements, in addition to the JCWS and its recent enhancements for more flexible offerings. Based on JDAMIS data, about 55 percent of JPME-II graduates were consistently from the JCWS; SSSs produced about 25 percent of the graduates, with the balance of almost 20 percent accomplished at SJSs (see Table 3.2). As these graduates achieve their JQO designation, the percentage of SSS graduates are increasing slightly over time (see Figure 4.4). Distinctions between JPME-II institutions for JQO designates also vary considerably by service and grade—Air Force, Army, and Marine Corps O-6 JQOs make greatest use of SSSs, and Navy O-6 JQOs make greatest use of the JCWS (Figure 4.8). For the junior field grade (O-5 and O-4) JQOs, the JCWS was the dominant JPME-II provider.

Given the differences in program duration between SJSs and SSSs (ten months) and the JCWS (ten weeks), various constituencies are beginning to question the equivalence and quality of strategic joint educational outcomes. Such questions are beyond the scope of this study, but it is evident that the JCWS satisfies a considerably high portion of the JPME-II educational requirements as currently defined, addresses both O-4 and O-5 educational needs that cannot be satisfied by either an SJS or SSS as currently configured, offers a range of flexibilities in terms of geographical satellite and hybrid offerings, and has a diversity of students and faculty that is difficult for all SSSs to consistently achieve as they are currently executed. Similarly, we expect that modifications to current JPME-II offerings would have greater differential impact on the reserve component although this was not an explicit focus area of this study.

The Trend Toward JPME-II Completion After Joint Assignment

While we did not explicitly explore the accomplishment of JPME-I, we did note that direct entry waivers were a rare exception, authorized strictly on a case-by-case basis. (Such waivers allow JPME-I to be completely waived or taken out of sequence relative to JPME-II.) Therefore, in cases where officers receive JPME-II education after the completion of their S-JDA tours, they are relying completely on their JPME-I instruction as the basis for and context to performing in joint assignments. As is shown in Figure 5.1, this reliance on only intermediate JPME was the case in 65 percent, 41 percent, and 37 percent of JQOs who completed their JPME-II requirement at SSSs, SJSs, and the JCWS, respectively, after their joint duty assignments. These trends have increased over the ten-year period that we examined (see Figure 5.2) and offer support for the anecdotal concerns raised by joint organization leaders who have lamented the strategic ability of officers to deal with a range of joint requirements. The CJCS's Process for Accreditation of Joint Education should examine this issue as an item of special interest.

JPME Experience Sequencing

As we noted in Chapter One, nothing in law or policy dictates to the services the required sequencing of JPME-II graduation and assignment to a joint billet. There is a preference that joint education precede assignment, but it is evident from trends that the services do not approach JPME-II as a prerequisite for a standard joint tour. We consistently heard from each of the services that the sequencing of education and assignment was determined not by the leadership intent of education preparing an officer for the rigors of a joint assignment but rather by "timing and availability" for both the individual officer and the good of the service or joint organization.

The wide variety of venues for JPME-II allows the services to accomplish joint education in patterns largely unique to each service.

- *Before or during a joint assignment.* The Air Force and Marine Corps most consistently accomplished JPME-II prior to or early in a joint tour.
- *Before a joint assignment, if possible, but much later if necessary.* The Army placed some officers into the JCWS before or during a joint tour, but also educated a large percentage of JQOs at SSSs much later in their career.
- *Whenever seats are available at the JCWS.* The Navy placed a disproportionate percentage of its officers into the JCWS, regardless of grade, reflecting the ease by which it could fill unused JCWS seats with officers assigned to the Norfolk, Virginia, area.

Joint education is a lever that the services can control in that the timing of education rests on service decisions and priorities. Because law and policy do not serve as a forcing mechanism for joint education timing, the services use pathways that support service objectives. When the service uses JQO attainment as a screening mechanism, as in the Air Force and Marine Corps, joint education often occurs near in time to a joint assignment. When SSS selection outweighs the importance of JQO attainment, joint education occurs later in an officer's career through the SSS, as in the Army. When joint education must be accomplished in as little time as possible, as in the Navy, the JCWS becomes the only viable alternative to the service.

Primary Drivers for Joint Qualified Officer Production

The Question of Preparations Needed for Assignments

The original intent of the GNA was to increase the quality, stability, and experience of officers assigned to joint organizations; this, in turn, would improve joint outcomes. As discussed previously, this direction is accomplished through the combination of joint education and joint duty assignments.

The joint education requirement reflects a career-long commitment to an officer PME that spans from precommissioning to the most senior general and flag officer ranks. Such education requires balancing both service and joint offerings. This obligation to progressively gain proficiency in joint matters through instruction is a fundamental pedagogical concept consistent with the ever increasing requirements and demands expected by senior joint leaders of their assigned officers. Through CJCSI 1800.01E, the Joint Staff has detailed the standards, learning areas, and objectives that define the JPME programs for officers to be successful in joint assignments. These specifications cover all ranks of field grade officers. Through the completion of successive levels of PME and JPME, field grade officers are prepared for the rigors of joint assignments.

Additionally, joint duty assignments reflect the demands of all joint commands and organizations. The demands are expressed in terms of the JDAL, which is validated to not only reflect joint billet requirements but also the grades necessary to perform these duties. The JDAL is heavily weighted toward requirements for the more junior ranks of field grade officers. Across all services, the distribution of grades are approximately 45 percent O-4s, 35 percent O-5s, and 20 percent O-6s.[4]

Developing both service and joint expertise (i.e., the combination of both joint education and a joint duty assignment) within the constraint of a fixed career length is challenging. As a result, the preferred order of education and then assignment is not always possible. As the services increasingly seek to accomplish JPME through senior institutions, postassignment education will progressively become the de facto standard (as opposed to the exception), and thereby JPME-I and intermediate service PME will be the only instructional preparations for the preponderance of O-5 assignments and all O-4 positions. This raises a fundamental question regarding the educational prerequisites, if any, and preparations needed to successfully perform the duties of joint assignments, especially for junior personnel. Feedback from senior joint leadership over time will be essential to assess the impact of this transition to greater use of senior institutions. Again, this topic should be a focus item for the Process for Accreditation of Joint Education, with explicit attention on the performance outcomes of the more junior field grade officers.

Service Manning Guidance for Joint Assignments

Continuing to acknowledge that joint duty assignments remain an important component of an officer's development, the services stated that joint manpower demands have outpaced available officer inventories. To sustain readiness levels and to balance service manpower inventories with the need for joint requirements and officer development, the services have developed guidance that prioritizes personnel fill rates. Relative to past years, this guidance typically has adjusted joint manning levels down slightly, but they still remain at relatively high levels. Some services have also made differentia-

---

[4]   Donald J. Cymrot and Gregg Schell, *Sizing the Joint Duty Assignment List (JDAL)*, Arlington, Va.: Center for Naval Analysis, DRM-2017-U-014879, 2017.

tions between priorities for various categories of joint requirements (e.g., manning at CCMDs versus Joint Staff).

Service Compliance Driven by Binding Constraints

The original GNA legislation had two binding constraints that sought to define measures of congressional intent and to ensure that the services sufficiently complied: (1) comparable promotion rates for officers in joint assignments with officers in service headquarters, and (2) JQO designation prior to consideration for promotion to general or flag officer. The comparable promotion rate constraint was modified with the April 2018 JOM policy update and is now only reported to OSD. Conversely, general and flag officer promotion consideration has only been reinforced in the sense that waivers associated with prior education or experiential requirements are rarely granted. In fact, one service for two consecutive years had O-6s who had not fully completed the JQO designation process removed from the general officer consideration list. In both cases, waivers were denied. It is evident from the JQO trend results that reported metrics provide a strong forcing function to drive service behaviors and policies.

There is no longer a question about the criticality of jointness being central to the success of any mission conducted by DoD. The department has made tremendous advances in this regard since the initial passage of the GNA. Advancements have resulted from investments in the career-long development of officers to be proficient in joint matters and from the revision of associated policies. This research has contributed to understanding the past and current state of joint qualifications for active component field grade officers and serves as a foundation and baseline for understanding, designing, and assessing future personnel policy changes that benefit the joint force, military services, and individual officers.

Bibliography

Booz Allen Hamilton, *Independent Study of Joint Officer Management and Joint Professional Military Education*, McLean, Va.: Booz Allen Hamilton, 2003.

Chairman of the Joint Chiefs of Staff Instruction (CJCSI) 1301.01F, *Joint Individual Augmentation Procedures*, November 17, 2014. As of February 28, 2019:
https://www.jcs.mil/Portals/36/Documents/Library/Instructions/1301_01.pdf?ver=2016-02-05 -175004-953

———— 1800.01E, *Officer Professional Military Education Policy (OPMEP)*, May 29, 2015a. As of February 28, 2019:
https://www.jcs.mil/Portals/36/Documents/Doctrine/education/cjcsi1800_01e.pdf?ver=2017-12-29 -142206-877

———— 1330.05A, *Joint Officer Management Program Procedures*, December 15, 2015b. As of February 28, 2019:
https://www.jcs.mil/Portals/36/Documents/Library/Instructions/1330_05a.pdf?ver=2016-02-05 -175005-720

Chairman of the Joint Chiefs of Staff Memorandum CM-1081-10, *Joint Qualified Officer (Level III) Requirements*, June 8, 2010.

———— CM-1084-14, *Program for Joint Professional Military Education Phase I Equivalent Credit*, June 27, 2014.

Cymrot, Donald J., and Gregg Schell, *Sizing the Joint Duty Assignment List (JDAL)*, Arlington, Va.: Center for Naval Analysis, DRM-2017-U-014879, 2017.

Deputy Assistant Secretary of the Army—Budget, "Budget Materials," webpage, undated. As of April 26, 2019:
https://www.asafm.army.mil/offices/bu/content.aspx?what=BudgetMaterials

Fenty, Linda, *The Joint Staff Officer Report*, Washington, D.C.: Joint Staff J7 / Joint Force Division, 2008.

Harrell, Margaret C., Harry J. Thie, Sheila Nataraj Kirby, Al Crego, Danielle M. Varda, and Thomas Sullivan, *A Strategic Approach to Joint Officer Management: Analysis and Modeling Results*, Santa Monica, Calif.: RAND Corporation, MG-886-OSD, 2009. As of March 13, 2019:
https://www.rand.org/pubs/monographs/MG886.html

Joint Chiefs of Staff, *Joint Personnel Support*, Washington, D.C.: Joint Chiefs of Staff, Joint Publication 1-0, 2016.

Joint Staff J1, Directorate for Manpower and Personnel, *Problem Statement: Joint Officer Management (JOM) Modernization, Version 2.5*, Washington, D.C.: Joint Staff J1, August 7, 2014.

————, *Fiscal Year 2016 Joint Officer Management Annual Report*, Washington, D.C.: Joint Staff J1, April 3, 2017.

Joint Staff J1, Directorate for Manpower and Personnel / Joint Officer Management Office, *Joint Chiefs of Staff Joint Duty Assignment Management Information System, Volume 1—Files*, Washington, D.C.: Joint Staff J1, undated.

Joint Staff J7, Joint Force Development, *Joint Qualification Report, Fiscal Year 2018, 3rd Quarter*, Washington, D.C.: Joint Staff J1, June 30, 2018. As of August 28 2018: https://wss.apan.org/s/JSOFUN/jom_jqs/SitePages/Home.aspx

Kamarck, Kristy, *Goldwater-Nichols and the Evolution of Officer Joint Professional Military Education*, Washington, D.C.: Congressional Research Service, R44340, 2016.

Kirby, Sheila Nataraj, Al Crego, Harry J. Thie, Margaret C. Harrell, Kimberly Curry Hall, and Michael S. Tseng, *Who Is "Joint"? New Evidence from the 2005 Joint Officer Management Census Survey*, Santa Monica, Calif.: RAND Corporation, TR-349-OSD, 2006. As of March 12, 2019: https://www.rand.org/pubs/technical_reports/TR349.html

Murdock, Clark A., Michèle A. Flournoy, Kurt M. Campbell, Pierre A. Chao, Julianne Smith, Anne A. Witkowsky, and Christine E. Wormuth, *Beyond Goldwater-Nichols: U.S. Government and Defense Reform for a New Strategic Era—Phase 2 Report*, Washington, D.C.: Center for Strategic and International Studies, July 2005.

Porter, Charles H., Kory Fierstine, S. Craig Goodwyn, and David Gregory, *Joint Officer Management Modernization Analysis of Alternatives (AoA)*, Washington, D.C.: Center for Naval Analyses, 2017.

Public Law 99-433, Goldwater-Nichols Department of Defense Reorganization Act of 1986, October 1, 1986. As of August 14, 2018: https://history.defense.gov/Portals/70/Documents/dod_reforms/Goldwater-NicholsDoDReordAct1986.pdf

RAND Corporation, *Realigning the Stars: A Methodology for Reviewing Active Component General and Flag Officer Requirements*, Santa Monica, Calif.: RAND Corporation, RR-2384-OSD, 2018. As of February 13, 2019: https://www.rand.org/pubs/research_reports/RR2384.html

Shaw, Ryan and Miriam Krieger, "Don't Leave Jointness to the Services: Preserving Joint Officer Development amid Goldwater-Nichols Reform," *War on the Rocks*, December 30, 2015. As of August 24, 2018: https://warontherocks.com/2015/12/dont-leave-jointness-to-the-services-preserving-joint-officer-development-amid-goldwater-nichols-reform/

Thie, Harry J., Margaret C. Harrell, Roland J. Yardley, Marian Oshiro, Holly Ann Potter, Peter Schirmer, and Nelson Lim, *Framing a Strategic Approach for Joint Officer Management*, Santa Monica, Calif.: RAND Corporation, MG-306-OSD, 2005. As of April 25, 2019: https://www.rand.org/pubs/monographs/MG306.html

U.S. Air Force Instruction 36-2301 Attachment 4, "Air Force Officer / Civilian SDE Fellowship (AFF) Program Descriptions," July 16, 2010. As of May 1, 2019: https://www.airuniversity.af.edu/Portals/10/AFFellows/documents/Fellowships-SDE.pdf

U.S. Air Force, Financial Management and Comptroller, "Air Force President's Budget FY20," webpage, undated. As of April 26, 2019: https://www.saffm.hq.af.mil/FM-Resources/Budget/

U.S. Army Combined Arms Center, *Senior Service College / Fellowship / Foreign School Information, AY 2012–2013*. Fort Leavenworth, Kan.: U.S. Army Combined Arms Center, 2012. As of October 12, 2018:
https://usacac.army.mil/cac2/IPO/repository/SSC_Schools_ Info_Catalog_AY12-13%5B1%5D.pdf

U.S. Army General Officer Management Office, Army Brigadier General Public Resumes, 2018. As of May 1, 2019:
https://www.gomo.army.mil

U.S. Army Regulation 350-1, Army Training and Leader Development, 2017.

United States Code, Title 10, Subtitle A, General Military Law, Part II, Personnel, Chapter 38, Joint Officer Management. As of February 28, 2019:
https://www.law.cornell.edu/uscode/text/10/subtitle-A/part-II/chapter-38

———, Title 10, Subtitle A, General Military Law, Part III, Training and Education, Chapter 107, Professional Military Education. As of February 28, 2019:
https://www.law.cornell.edu/uscode/text/10/subtitle-A/part-III/chapter-107

U.S. Congress, 109th Cong., 2nd Sess., *John Warner National Defense Authorization Act for Fiscal Year 2007: Conference Report to Accompany H.R. 5122*, Washington, D.C.: U.S. Government Printing Office, Report 109-702, 2006. As of August 23, 2019:
https://www.congress.gov/109/crpt/hrpt702/CRPT-109hrpt702.pdf

U.S. Department of Defense Instruction (DoDI) 1312.1-1, *Occupational Conversion Index: Enlisted/Officer/Civilian*, March 2001. As of February 28, 2019:
https://www.esd.whs.mil/Portals/54/Documents/DD/issuances/dodm/131201i.pdf

——— 1300.19, *DoD Joint Officer Management (JOM) Program*, April 3, 2018. As of February 28, 2019:
https://www.esd.whs.mil/Portals/54/Documents/DD/issuances/dodi/130019p.pdf?ver=2018-04-03 -114842-923

U.S. Department of the Navy, "Budget Materials," webpage, undated. As of April 26, 2019:
http://www.secnav.navy.mil/fmc/fmb/Pages/Fiscal-Year-2019.aspx

U.S. Government Accountability Office, *Actions Needed to Implement DoD Recommendations for Enhancing Leadership Development*, Washington, D.C.: U.S. Government Accountability Office, GAO-14-29, 2013.

U.S. House of Representatives, Committee on Armed Services, *Report of the Panel on Military Education of the One Hundredth Congress*, Washington, D.C.: U.S. Government Printing Office, April 21, 1989. As of September 4, 2018:
http://www.au.af.mil/au/awc/awcgate/congress/skelton1989/skelton.pdf

U.S. House of Representatives, Committee on Armed Services, Subcommittee on Oversight and Investigations, *Another Crossroads? Professional Military Education Two Decades After the Goldwater-Nichols Act and the Skelton Panel*, Washington, D.C.: House Armed Services Committee, April 2010. As of August 24, 2018:
http://www.dtic.mil/dtic/tr/fulltext/u2/a520452.pdf

Watkins, Brian T., *Are We Too Dumb to Execute Our Own Doctrine? An Analysis of Professional Military Education, Talent Management, and Their Ability to Meet the Intent of the Capstone Concept for Joint Operations*, Norfolk, Va.: Joint Forces Staff College, Joint Advanced Warfighting School, 2016.